This book is dedicated to the memory of my mother, Marjory, and to my sister, Tiffany, my mother-in-law, Marguerite, and my daughters, Diana, Dawn, and Daniele--women I most love.

Note from the Publisher

All scriptural references are from the King James Version.

Indeed, this book is for all Christian women, in America and abroad. The unique aspect about this publication is that the testimonies are by Christian women who all happen to be Americans and of African descent. Their testimonies should encourage every reader, male or female, to share in the openness and beauty of each message.

Table of Contents

ACKNOWLEDGMENTS   i-ii
FOREWORD   iii
INTRODUCTION   iv-viii
PREFACE   ix-xi

Chapter One--A Bicycle Ride To Remember   1-5
(experiencing a coma and recovery)

Chapter Two--The Teen Years
by April Washington Goodwin   6-12
(experiencing an illness as a teen)

Chapter Three--80 Years Young
by Christine Weedon   13-19
(experiencing many challenges)

Chapter Four--Remembering the 60s
by Roberta Dowdy   20-28
(experiencing the 60s as a young mother)

Chapter Five--A Minister's Wife
by H. Susie Ezell   29-39
(experiencing ministering abroad and in US)

Chapter Six--A Missionary For The Lord
by Beverly Frowner   40-49
(experiencing being a missionary)

Chapter Seven--Changed Inside And Out
by Diana Hammuck   50-58
(experiencing the causes and effects of giving up one's children for adoption)

Chapter Eight--A Letter Written To God
by Ruby Fields   59-68
(experiencing the healing power of God)

Chapter Nine--Unequally Yoked   69-75
by Gloria Brown
(experiencing the joys and challenges of marriage)

Chapter Ten--In His Time   76-84
by Jacquelin Wright
(experiencing the challenges of being a single)

Chapter Eleven--Dreams Do Come True   85-95
by Arlene Thomas
(experiencing the loss and gain of the material and the triumph of the spiritual during good and bad times)

Chapter Twelve--He Looked Beyond My Faults   96-107
by Terylle Lavender
(experiencing the challenge of being an unwed mother)

Chapter Thirteen--Oh How I Love Him So   108-120
by Marjory Washington Patrick
(experiencing the Lord in interracial settings)

Chapter Fourteen--Ye Are "A Living Epistle"   121
by You!
(experiencing the commitment by you, the reader)

Being Black
is a gift,
unique and challenging.
Being a woman
is fulfilling,
so many things to do,
to be, to become.
Being a Christian
is joyously struggling,
destined to be like Him.
Can you imagine being all three?
What a way to be!

Reflections of Christian Women

ACKNOWLEDGMENTS

I am most grateful to "the only wise God" and my Saviour, Jesus Christ, for the mercy and grace to complete this book. I stand in awe of His design and sovereignty in creating me to be an African-American woman. One of my favorite Bible verses is Hebrews 6:10, "For God is not unfair. How can He forget the way you used to show your love for Him--and still do by helping His children" (Living Bible).

I am also eternally grateful to my former pastors, Reverend King A. Butler and Dr. Raymond H. Saxe for their nurturing, shepherding, and, oft times, painful criticism which reminded me, things worth doing are worth doing right. Their standards often appeared unattainable but became just the target to aim for. To members of both the Bible Baptist Church and the Fellowship Bible Church, I am indebted for their obedience to God's Word. Hebrews 10:24; 25 reminds "Let us consider one another to provoke unto love and good works...exhorting one another and so much more as ye see the day approaching." Their encouragement and prayers meant much.

To Beverly Jones of Victory Glory workshops who authored *Black Woman: God Has Not Forgotten You*, thanks for being there to say, "You can do all things through Christ who strengthens you" when I felt I could not complete this ten-year old project.

To my four wonderful children, DJ, Diana, Dawn, and Daniele, thanks for your sacrifices. To family members who wondered, "What are you doing NOW," thanks for your endurance, and to my husband, Dave, my undying thanks for always believing in me.

May God repay Winnifred Northcross, Tumbi Soremekun, Diana Patrick, Jean Balakovich, Michelle Thomas, Jack & Carolyn Brandmeier, and B & J for the emotional and financial support.

Previously, I wondered many things when I read the acknowledgment pages of other books. I now know, thank you, are not words enough to express what is felt for the input and hard work of those who help to see a book to completion. Thank you, Rebecca Osaigbovo, who has authored "*Chosen Vessels: Women of Color Keys to Change,*" for your intercessory prayers. Thank you, Kim Reid, for your hours of typing and sacrifice, and, for the professional content editing skills of Dee Dee Worthington, I am eternally grateful.

I am also honored to include the God-given artistic drawings of the late June Schauer and Diana Patrick.

A final word of thanks goes to the many saints of God whom I met here on the South African shores. What beautiful women of God! It would take another book just to mention them all by name. To Sandra S., Sandra Q., Mary, Lilly, and Charmaine, special thanks for their prayers and encouragement.

FOREWORD

Here in an easy to read style is the witness of a community of African-American Christian women. They are of varied backgrounds and age levels. Their witness is a testimony to the grace of God. I can see this book, REFLECTIONS OF CHRISTIAN WOMEN, meeting several needs. For we live in a day when much is said to confuse the faith of so many Christians. This book can make clear the Christian faith to the non-Christian. It can serve to strengthen the faith of Christians. And in this book can be found the challenge for a basis for personal faith in the Lord Jesus Christ as Saviour and also as the provider for every need.

I commend sister Marjie Washington Patrick for the labor and love in letting the Lord use her and others to compile this book. I trust that it will have wide distribution and acceptance as a witness for our Lord and Savior, Jesus Christ.

                                        Pastor King A. Butler,
                                        I Corinthians 3:9a

Pastor Butler has written several book forewords published by Moody Press, and he has written several Gospel tracts.

INTRODUCTION

Scores of material has been written about the African-American Woman from Sojourner Truth's *Ain't I A Woman*, Mattie Griffith's *The Autobiography of a Female Slave, 1857*, Toni Cade's *Anthology, The Black Woman*, Lerner's *The Black Woman in White America*, and Sharon Hauley & Rosalyn Terborg-Penn's *The Afro-American Woman*, and other books and publications such as *Essence*, all providing a positive definition and perspective to Black womanhood. I know not whether these authors profess a personal relationship with Jesus Christ or if their intent in writing were to give a Christian perspective of women of color. If I hold a microscope to view life, my first lens is from a Christian perspective, how does the Word of God, how does Christ Himself view what I am seeing? Each one of us brings to any given life scope, a unique perspective which is a combination of our environment, education, past experiences, and a myriad of other factors. From a variety of perspectives, volumes have been written by and about the African-American woman.

Today, I am elated to walk into Christian bookstores and finally be able to see material that displays the work of people of color in Christendom. As a young girl, I asked my mother why Black people were not on the covers of printed material in Christian bookstores? Here in the 1990s I am blessed by long time classics that enrich the Christian experience. These books are evangelical, filled with fundamental biblical truths, but the life examples are not typical or specific to the African-American woman's experience. One must admit that this is long overdue and yet not exhausted, for no other racial, ethnic, or religious group of females in the United States, aside from the Native American and Hispanic women, have undergone as much degradation, stereotyping, and actual punishment as the African-American woman in America.

We have been seen as submissive "Aunt Jemimas" with grinning faces and fat embracing arms, leering buxom wenches dependent on welfare, or hard core, self-reliant male bashers. Since 1619 when our ancestors were brought to the U.S., we have lived through conditions of cruelties so horrible, so bizarre, so different than the scores of women of other ethnic groups who have suffered in other ways. The usual cultural image of the African-American woman in America is that of a domineering type who rules the family, including her husband if she has one! Yes, we are aware of a variety of factors which interact to create a disproportionate number of female-headed households in the African-American community. More than half of the African-American families headed by a woman live in poverty, having a median family income below $3,000 a year. The question quick to ask next is, "Where is the African-American male and why is he not taking care of his family?" Unemployment rates have long been twice as high among African-American men as among white men. This often leads the family to depend on the ever depleting welfare system to meet its needs. This system has made it a condition for receipt of certain types of aid that the male be absent from the home in order for the women along with their children to receive financial assistance. Welfare in the U.S. is definitely linked to racist oppression.

The total ratio of female-headed households is another element contributing to the familiar absence of the African-American male. There are about 85 African-American males for every 100 African-American females. Death rates for young African-American males are much higher than for any other sex/race group. There is a large number of African-American male prisoners. The percentage of African-Americans within the prison population is higher than any other population. In large metropolitan cities, as many as 90% of the county jails' inhabitants are African-American. It is estimated that there are more African-Americans in prison than in college. Having taught in three of Michigan's prison facilities, I left the classes saying to myself, "No wonder I find so few brothers on the outside; there are so many in prison!" While there I'd often voice, "Your body might be behind these bars, but your mind isn't, so let's get busy with the course work before us."

Considering these spiraling statistics and the numerous facts, I fail to mention here, many African-American women feel they don't need a man or are apathetic to issues which affect all of us. Even in a time of open mindedness and brotherly love, how many African-American women stand wondering why they're left rejected by African-American men who have run to open arms of white women. The issue is not whether interracial relationships are wrong or right--the real issue is answering the question, why the rejection?

The travail of the African-American woman has spanned two continents and four centuries. The shadows of slavery, the scars of the civil rights battles, social role shifts, and myriads of problems cause circumstances which force African-American women to be strong and self-reliant in order to achieve the survival of the African-American community. Highly visible are two of Satan's most effective tools -- divide and conquer.

When the reality of the African-American woman's history is understood, it is made clear why some African-American women are and need be more concerned with the elevation of their men than in liberation for themselves. Since white society has deprived African-American men of equal job and educational opportunities, many African-American women know what it is like to be equal to men and have no desire to join movements for the elevation of women. In my own life, for example, securing financial assistance or entrance into certain education programs became more accessible to me than for my husband. As an African-American female, I fulfilled two minority quotas in one--black and female. Somewhere in our struggles of living in an Eurocentric culture that promotes many values that are not consistent with the word of God, we have lost the essential ingredients necessary for binding us as African-American men and woman together in love. The culture in which we live has defined these concepts of our identity: definitions of our ideals, attitudes, behaviors, roles, and responsibilities. Yet God still has an ideal, an image He wants .... what He predestined the African-American female to be for His glory.

Over the years, in my employment as a secondary education teacher, a telemarketor for the University of Michigan Institute for Social Research, instructor in Michigan's prison facilities, and as a community college professor, I have interacted with a variety of women. Even as a young girl, I would accompany my mother who spent time ministering to the spiritual needs of a variety of women. I'd like to introduce you to some of these women. Their testimonies were by no means selected because they are extraordinary; millions like them have similar defeats and even greater victories. As you read these and enter the lives of these Christian African-American women, I trust you will not focus on them, but on the God who longs to live and work through each of us.

You may be reading this book because you are seeking answers to the dilemmas and problems facing African-American people in general and the African-American Christian woman in particular. Some may expect to find forever sought formulas to give them a new sense of direction as a Christian African-American woman. Some African-American men may read this and want truly to understand and become involved in the shaping and healing of the African-American Christian woman. I would pray that non Blacks reading this book would empathize with the similarities and come away with a better understanding of the particularities of the African-American Christian woman in order to participate in the healing of the whole body. "And whether one member suffer, all the members suffer with it..." (I Cor. 12:26).

"I have enough problems of my own," you might say. "Why should I care about the problems of an ordinary African-American woman?" Yes, your hurt, your sin affects our hurt, our sin, and vice versa. None of us has fully arrived. Yet, each of us has been given gifts for the perfecting of the saints, for the work of the ministry, for the edifying of the body of Christ: Till we all come in the unity of the faith, and of the knowledge of the Son of God, perfect in Christ (Ephesians 4:12-13). Others, of course, will simply be curious to see what the Christian African-American woman and her peers have gone through. Foremost, I hope you will see a part of yourself and find it refreshing to read a work on the Evangelical Christian African-American woman which does not indict, but allows us to see ourselves as God would have His image reflected in the Christian African-American woman.

We are each created with a purpose--destined to be like Him. "In whom He did foreknow, He also did predestine to be conformed to the image of His son"(Romans 8:29). Reading about these African-American women should cause you to think of others who have had similar experiences. Maybe you are going through similar experiences. How have these women trusted the Lord through these life experiences? How are you trusting the Lord in your experiences? What elements need to be put off or put on in order for them, for you, to become more Christ like? Questions for discussion have been included with each testimony as suggestions for group interaction.

How can you share in another Christian sister's struggles or joys until we all come in the unity of the faith? As we go through life, whose reflection do we see, Christ's?

PREFACE

TESTIMONY (tes'te-mo-ne) Open declaration of faith; evidence; proof. Why share a testimony someone might ask? In the 24th chapter of the book of Acts, we find an excellent answer to this question. Today in the 1990s as then 60 AD, we find ourselves as Christians in a world ready to accuse those of us who name the name of Christ (vs 2). Is there any validity to what we acclaim? Our accusers await, examining our lives, looking for evidence that would convict us of being a Christian (vs 8). At the same time, the world awaits and beckons for our response (vs 10). Paul cheerfully answered for himself. He knew there was a world around him and a generation yet future who needed to understand that Jesus is who He says He is in the lives of those who bear His name--Christian.

In Chapter 25 Paul realized there was a risk to let his testimony be known. Communication by nature is risky. Disclosure is even a greater risk. Then why was Paul so elated to tell his story (chapter 26)? Paul begins his story from the time of his youth and progresses with his testimony from that point until the point in time when he meets Jesus for himself face to face.

We share our testimonies because we have a story to tell. The story really isn't about us but rather what God has done for, in, and through us. Like the Psalmist in Ps 108:1, we cry, "O God, my heart is fixed: I will sing and give praise, even with my glory" (The Hebrew word used for glory is tongue). We have a story to tell that the angels can not tell--we've been redeemed!. The heavens declare God's glory and all creation expresses God's wonders. Animals bark, roar, grunt, send out sonar signals, and non-verbal messages. We as humans, men and women, boys and girls, created in the image of God are the only ones who can speak in intelligible, symbolic, abstract speech. "I will sing of the mercies of the Lord forever: With my mouth will I make known thy faithfulness to all generations" (Ps. 89:1).

A personal testimony is an effective witness. The testimony doesn't have to be dramatic. As Christians our testimonies need to articulate the assurance, express the transformation of the work of Christ in our lives, and portray obedience to God who said, "Let the redeemed of the Lord say so!!!"

We don't express our testimonies for any glory of our own but rather out of concern for the listeners. I have attended many a funeral and have seen sons and daughters left wondering, hoping, thinking mother-father was a Christian. How sad! The world, those close to us need to know God changes lives. Most definitely our walk needs to match our talk. It is marvelous to be at home-going services of the redeemed. Sons and daughters, husbands and wives rejoice knowing that their loved one has passed from death to life. These confident ones rejoice having witnessed the life of their loved one as having a testimony which matched the life they lived. They sorrow, yet not like those who have no hope. They rejoice knowing that their loved one is absent from the body but present with the Lord! They are encouraged and comforted by the testimony the believer held. Yes, we, through our lives might be the only Bible some people may ever read. Our testimony might be the only testimony someone ever heard told.

I look at telling a testimony this way, too. How often do we as Christians get to tell the Lord, "I love you Lord. Thank-you for what you've done for me?" If I tell Him one more time it wouldn't be a time too many. Some Christians live their lives without telling their testimony. How tragic if at judgment day, a relative, neighbor, co-worker would stand embarking a Christless eternity having to say, "You could have told me".

Paul was obedient. He shared his testimony. King Agrippa heard the testimony and was almost persuaded. Almost won't be good enough. "Behold now is the accepted time; behold, now is the day of salvation" (II Cor, 6:2).

I am certain that there is someone in your life or even a stranger who needs to hear your testimony, how you personally came to know Christ. Are you certain you have a testimony to tell? If you have truly been redeemed by the blood of the Lamb, then you have a story to tell. I am grateful for the opportunity to include the testimonies of these dozen women. I could have included the stories of more women, but I had to stop at some point. At the end of the book, I have included pages for you to write out you own personal testimony. If you are sharing this book in a group setting, be sure to discuss the similarities and differences that exist in your life and the lives of those shared here. Take time to share your own personal testimony with those in your group.

We've a story to tell to the nations that shall turn their hearts to the right. A story of truth and mercy, a story of peace and light....

Reflections of Christian Women

Chapter One

Chapter One
A BICYCLE RIDE TO REMEMBER

by Annie Watson

My name is Annie Lela Watson. As a baby I always went to church, and I grew spiritually in successive years of Sunday school classes. I was five years old when I accepted Jesus Christ as my personal Saviour. Soon after, I was baptized as a public witness to my faith.

Now it was time for me to live for the Lord. I started as a service to God, singing in my church's junior and youth choirs. I took private piano and violin lessons, and attended related workshops and camps. My church gave me the opportunity to play my instruments for Sunday school and special worship services. Having a part in the services really helped me grow as a young Christian.

I look forward to the Sundays when the Sunbeam or junior choir members put on our white blouses and blue skirts. We gathered in the back room after Sunday school for prayer and final instructions. The title of our selections were printed in the morning bulletin. Sister Bessie Wooden, our directress, gave so much to the Lord as she faithfully worked with us each week. Bible study and Christian camps encouraged me in my relationship with the Lord.

One sunny, summer day, I had an experience which helped me become a more committed young Christian. I just received a new yellow bike that I was so proud of. "Be careful", my mother reminded me. There was a long, steep street. I couldn't stop the bike. I went into the street. I was hit by a truck. Although I was in a coma and in serious condition for two weeks, God took care of me. I'm told my mother stayed at my side and prayed and my family (daddy, Mary, Pug, and Thomas) prayed for me at home. I now know that my whole church was praying for God's will in my life and for my family's. The accident was reported in the newspaper. God must have touched the heart of the salesman. Because to my surprise, I received a new bike from the store. I received many cards, phone calls, flowers, and other gifts. However, the greatest gift God gave me at that time was life to continue here on earth.

It was a blessing to be able to walk again. I could still play from memory several songs, but one song in particular I could not remember. Unfortunately, the accident had affected my speech, as well as other parts of my brain.

In the hospital, there was a room with a piano. One day, as I touched the keys, I played the whole piece! It was a miracle from God! I was very thankful for what God had brought me through.

Fully recovered, I bounced back into all sorts of activities available to little girls. In school I had a desire to do my best in my studies. My parents got me involved in other extra-curricular activities with my piano and violin or Girl Scouts or other programs. I didn't dwell on the thoughts that entered my mind, but I always wondered why was I one of the only African-American girls in many of these activities? Where were so many of the other African-American children? I didn't let this feeling of being the only one of color stop me from gaining the experiences these activities and groups offered me. Voices would sometimes utter," you must think you're better; you must think you are white. You are an "Uncle Tom". I ignored these voices. I was welcomed and accepted into these activities and programs which appeared to be developed for white children. I do remember programs being available at the community center near where I lived but often lacked parental involvement, supervision, or funds to keep programs running. So even if I had to be the only one of color in these other groups, I would be because these became stepping stones where self-confidence and a positive self image could be built in me. These wholesome activities added direction to my life. They helped me learn and want to achieve. My parents attended these programs with me. So many young children had nothing constructive to do, no goals to reach for, no hope for their future. I shall always be grateful for the programs my parents supported me to be a part of. These helped give me direction and purpose as I learned, as a child, what a privilege it was to live for my Creator and Savior. When it is my turn to say a scripture verse at dinner, I recite Phillippians 4:13 "I can do all things through Christ that strengthens me."

"Suffer the little children to come unto me, and forbid them not: for of such is the kingdom of God." Mark 10: 14.

Annie's life is an example of how God can accomplish His purposes even in the life of a little child who is yielded to Him. Sunday school teachers should be encouraged to remain true to one's calling because God is faithful to allow fruit to be gleaned from this all-important ministry. There are young Black girls in puff hair balls, thick braids, or soft corn rolls, with the joy of the Lord in the face of tragedy, or tranquillity. God can be glorified through these young girls' lives. May God help us, as older Black women, to be examples, to help raise them, and to nurture them in the things of God.

We live in an age where young girls are exposed to what was once considered unimaginable. For example, a friend told me of one young girl, about the age of Annie, recently stayed home alone with her six year-old sister while her mother was off visiting in Chicago. Having only $5.00, she wondered whether to wash clothes at the Laundromat or to buy something for dinner.

A recent campaign slogan, "save the children" could be God's call for Christians to be available in the local church or community. Surely there are more young Black children who are willing to accept Christ as their own personal Saviour, and live obediently, to God's glory!

Above all, Annie's parents realized that God gave Annie to them. She was on loan to them, an investment, as it were, which would require interest. They understood the main responsibility did not lie with the church or the community programs. Annie's parents didn't send her to Sunday school; they were there with her. Relatives and neighbors did not take the main responsibility of Annie; as her parents, they did. Parents who by the grace of God follow the principles of God such as those found in Deuteronomy 6:6-7 "And these words, which I command thee this day, shall be in thine heart: And thou (parents) shall teach them diligently unto thy children, and shalt talk of them when thou sittest in thine house, and when thou walkest by the way, and when thou liest down, and when thou risest up." These will be parents, indeed, having children whose lives are filled with hope and good success.

FOR DISCUSSION:

#1   What are 3 main problems facing young children today?

#2   Specifically, how can parents be part of the solution?

#3   Are there obstacles in your church or community programs which hinder the help so desperately needed to families with young children?

#4   As a parent of a young child, how have you neglected even in small ways, the God-given responsibilities which accompany the privilege of having a child? What concrete steps can you take to make a difference?

#5   Statistics show that 85% of any one making a decision for Christ does so between the ages of 4-14. How does this impress the significance that raising and influencing children is very important?

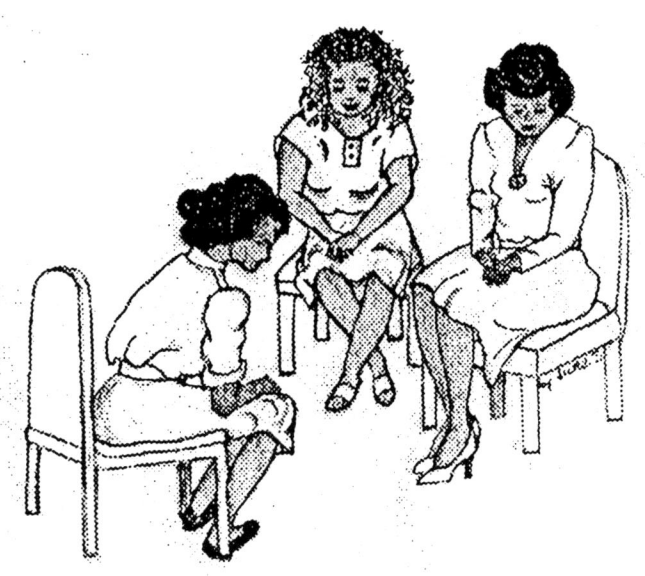

Chapter Two

Chapter Two
THE TEEN YEARS

by April Washington Goodwin

Just one more year of those long, hard, but joyful years as a teenager! At nineteen, I can say I'm a proud young Christian Black woman. Each year has brought new and different dimensions into my life. I can remember when I longed to be "sweet 16!" Even though I was a "slim jim," I wanted to be noticed by all the girls and guys. Funny, how being accepted is so important to teenagers.

We're striving for independence on one hand and simultaneously asking for love on the other. We're asking for discipline, not just punishment. We want fair, consistent limits, rules, and guidelines. We want to be accepted for who and what we are becoming, not what parents want us to be. We want parents who will be themselves good examples. We are looking for good models, and, if they are not found in the house, we'll find them on the streets.

Ok, so statistics and charts show between the ages of 14-19 the influence of peers is the greatest, but these findings do not show we are still really crying out for parents and family to be our greatest influence. I am so grateful to have had grandparents, aunts, uncles, cousins, and siblings who shared a "real" sense of family. Big deals and grand celebrations were made over new family arrivals. Each of us were made proud to be a part of both my paternal and maternal families.

We'd join the whole clan for Saturday night chili and a few hands of bid whiz. On Sunday mornings we could be found worshipping together in church. It is in these family social settings with my family where I learned to have fun, wholesome interaction. This is what made it easy for me to steer away from settings other teens find themselves in...the drug scenes, the alcohol scenes, the sex scenes and all the after painful scenes. Did I live in a dream world? Was I over protected? Was it that I never faced temptations other teens face today? Believe me these scenes were no secret; I was not immune to their temptation. I could read the headlines: "Teenage Pregnancy Rises to Epidemic, Each Year 1 Million Teenage Girls Get Pregnant"; "Crimes Committed by Black Teens Rises to Epidemic Proportions"; Each Day in America 13 Teens Kill Themselves". These scenes also found themselves in my own family circles; teen pregnancy, war with drugs, and suicide attempts. How did I cope? How did I escape?

I am not presenting myself faultless, a "Miss Goody-Two Shoes." That would be hypercritical. I Corinthians 10:13 tells us "there is no temptation taken you but such as is common to man: but God is faithful, who will not suffer you to be tempted above that ye are able; but will with the temptation also make a way to escape." Many teens need not go the road of distruction; there is a way of escape.

At the age of twelve, I walked down to the church altar to accept Christ as my personal Saviour. There were a few shouts heard from others in the pews, and tears were rolling down the faces of the ladies in front of me. I cried too, but it didn't stop me from making this public decision. It wasn't until later in my life I found out that others were crying tears of joy and happiness. Because with Christ by your side, there is abundant joy in life.

After my profession of faith, it seemed I was at the church every time the doors were open. I went to Sunday school and youth meetings and joined the junior usher board. My friends were there, too. But attending church was not a mere social hangout. I am thankful that I can say that even though there were troublesome times, where I have had to sort out the guidelines set by my parents, at least the rules were there. I didn't always make the right decisions, but the Lord always brought me back to the place of wanting to be obedient. God's way is so much better than most of the choices that a lot of teens make today.

The Lord promises blessings, real blessings, eternal blessings to those who obey His principles. The world promises false blessings, false hopes, and only immediate gratification...a quick fix. The world says try drugs; you'll have real highs.

That lie never tells you could be hooked for life and end up joining the ranks of millions who leave trails of devastation.

The world says try sex; it's your body; do what comes natural; besides, there are all kinds of protection available even without parental permission. But will the world tell you there is little protection from the violation you feel not being ready for premarital sex or the unwanted pregnancies, or life threatening diseases or the so subtle affects of flashbacks which will occur late in life, or the guilt and condemnation which could plague your life for years? The world won't tell you that you're really looking for love and intimacy and you'll settle for moments of pleasure playing Russian roulette with sex. Sure the world says, use a condom—safe sex is the key. But fails to tell you there is no condom for the soul.

During my early teen years, I found out that I had a sickle cell trait. Sickle cell is a blood disease primarily affecting Black people. A person having only the "trait" doesn't usually experience the usual severe pain, unless he/she is in a place of high elevation.

At the age of sixteen, without warning, I was confronted with a strange pain in my left side, which was finally diagnosed as sickling in the kidney. I couldn't understand why this disease affected primarily Black people, nor why having the trait was causing me pain. Needing a special kind of comfort, I turned to prayer, and my faith in the Lord. He helped me accept this development and helped me empathize with others who were in far greater, more painful situations. Perhaps others did not have a personal relationship with God and did not have His grace to sustain. Through these difficult times, God showed me that I was a very special person. I found pride in being myself and bearing my cross for Him.

I have learned more about the Lord through daily experiences and by reading His Word. I realize that He is the One who awakens me in the morning. Also, I "see" the Lord through my father when he sings God's songs. I think that a child is more likely to see God as Father if he/she sees godliness in his/her father. What an awesome responsibility God has given fathers

(Deuteronomy 6:6-9). Many a father will stand in judgment for having failed to comply with God's demands of fathers.

I "see" the Lord through my mother, too, especially when she teaches and plays gospels or hymns on the piano. Both my parents praise God's name. There were times when I was embarrassed to tell my friends that we were having family praise and worship. I was afraid they would laugh and tease, even though I know teens often secretly value these times.

One of my favorite Bible stories recalls some people who came to see Jesus, wanting to be healed, or blessed. After Jesus had blessed and healed many, they went away happy, but never bothered to say "thank you." There was only one who turned around and went back to give thanks to the Lord. Today, I want to be a teenager who says, "thank you, Lord, for allowing me to be a young Christian African-American. As I leave these teen years behind, one goal that will continue to lead the others. That goal is to one day hear my Saviour say, 'Well done, my good and faithful servant' ."

"I your servant have feared the Lord from my youth." 1 Kings 18:12

If you have a special calling to work with teenagers like April, consider yourself blessed. I have recorded in diaries all of my teen years so that I can look back and remember the struggles faced. I treasure most that God allowed me to have several close Christian teen friends. Christian teenagers need to bind together and help one another along the Christian journey.

I am forever grateful to Doris Chatman, Fletcher Lewis, Iverna Shelton, Beverly Frowner, and others who spent time ministering to teens like me. I am also indebted to Danny Dew, Anton Jacobs, and Dwayne and Kim Reid who were the youth workers in the lives of my own teenagers. May your church be encouraged to have a program that assists teens in their Christian walk. To those Christian teens who are yet holding up the banner of Christ keep on, it's worth it! Let no man despise thy youth. "But be thou an example of the believers, in word, in conversation, in charity, in spirit, in faith, in purity" (1 Timothy 4:12). Give your life for His glory!

Men and women, youth pastors, and even older teens who help out in Awana programs, choirs, child evangelism programs, Youth for Christ or other teen ministries, do not grow weary in well doing. The Lord has promise you will reap a harvest if you faint not (Gal. 6:9). It doesn't matter whether you are leading in programs with great numbers of children or few.

Many adults are failing miserably at their roles of parenting. We are also living in an age where little respect is given by young children and youth. Hideous crimes are being committed by children and to children. I guess I'd agree one of the biggest crimes is the one where children are raising children and youth are raising themselves.

An even greater crime is where those of us who know the way are not willing to participate in programs or give financially to programs which do. Others become so discouraged from the lack of support from church leaders and those in the congregations who throw up their hands saying there's little hope for this generation, not realizing the cry is loud and clear: "Help us; give us love and direction. Don't just tell the way, but show the way and go the way with us."

"Children are crying everyday. Drugs are taking them away. Children are crying all around, a solution must be found. Gangs are destroying our schools. No more interest in the Golden Rule. They took prayer out of the class. Tell me how long will this last? Yes, there is hope, Lord, there's hope. As long as Jesus is alive there is hope" (Mississippi Mass Children's Choir).

FOR DISCUSSION

#1   Why are so few adults willing to get involved in youth programs? What are some of the main fears?

#2   When youth are in trouble what can other youth or adults do to help?

#3 Name several youth you are quite proud of. What are the factors which are helping these youth succeed?

#4 In I Timothy 4:12 what command does Paul give to youth and why?

#5 Are church programs really unrelated to the needs of youth?

Chapter Three

Chapter Three
80 YEARS YOUNG

by Christine Weeden

My testimony is lengthy because I am an old woman. Seventy of my eighty plus years I have been trying each day to be a better Christian than the day before. There is nothing I'd rather do than serve my Lord and Master Jesus Christ! There is no place I'd rather be than in the house of the Lord!

I can remember (before I was five years-old) wanting to be a Christian. My father was in a play at his church called, "The Prodigal Son." He was the son. At rehearsal when he graveled for the swines' food, I cried so loudly they had to take me out. At home, later he explained the Bible story to me. He showed me the way to God. He said Jesus is the way back to the Father. I wanted to be a Christian. My father often read the Bible to us or the Sunday school lesson and explained it so we could understand.

I had a toy piano, and one day I stopped "banging" and began singing and playing, "Pharaoh and his host got drowned in the red sea." Only I was singing "dog gone it" instead of drowned. My mother rushed in and stopped me, explaining that I was never to say "dog gone it" in religious songs or in speaking of God. So I sang and played "O Mary Don't You Mom" and made sure I sang all the words as they were supposed to be. (To this day, I emphasize saying words distinctly when speaking or singing.)

When my father heard I could actually play, he asked me to play for him. I held back. He said, "You play that song for me, and I'll buy you a real piano on your seventh birthday." I played this song and quite a few more. Whenever we visited anyone who had a piano, all they had to do was hum or sing a song, and I could play it! I really enjoyed this.

When I was seven years-old, my dad said he didn't have enough money to get the piano. The Lord made a way out of no way. On Christmas Eve, A. A. Tiller brought my piano. My mother insisted that I practice often. She bought me a book at the "ten cent store." I found out that I knew the notes and keys. I kept this piano until the flood of '37. When we returned to our Kentucky home, only the sounding board was left standing. I cried like everything because my lovely piano was ruined.

Before this flood, I had joined church. I was nine years-old at the time. My parents felt I didn't know what this phrase, "join church," meant, so they would not let me be baptized, insisting that I must wait a year. The pastor and Sunday school superintendent tried to persuade them to let me be baptized, but they wouldn't. When the year was up, I told them I was going to be baptized with or without their permission; they gave in, and I gladly prepared to be baptized. This is still vivid in my memory. I knew it was my faith in the finished work of Jesus Christ on the cross of Calvary that saved me but baptism was a commandment that Christ gave, an outward sign symbolizing my regeneration through union with Christ, portraying His death, burial, and resurrection (Roman 6:3-4). I wanted to be obedient.

I served as substitute accompanist at any service whenever I was asked, Sunday school, morning and evening services on Sunday, B.T.U. weekly services, and when visiting sister churches. I sometimes played for vespers services at Simmons University, the Y.W.C.A., and a congregation church.

One afternoon, about 4:00 P.M., I was peeling potatoes for supper. A very bright light came from above through the kitchen door which was open. I turned to see where this light came from. It was daylight, but this shaft of light was much brighter. When my eyes finally adjusted to this light, I could see a white paper rolled like a graduation certificate, and there was a blue ribbon tied around it. I tried to reach it, but it was just beyond my reach. I began to cry and called my mother to come and see it. She came but could not see the light or the paper. When dad came home, I was still sobbing, but not afraid or sad. We told him what had happen, so they asked the pastor, the superintendent, and two deacons to come and talk with us. They also prayed with us. They said they had been praying for a church organist (our lovely organist had just recently died). They believed God was telling them to choose me! My parents gave their consent, and I was so happy I began to cry again. This was in 1918. I have been a pianist/organist from then until now. I knew I had a special talent from the Lord -- the ability to play anything and everything by ear. If this were truly a gift from God, shouldn't I use it only for God? If not, wouldn't that be like shouting on Sunday and shacking on Monday? Wouldn't that be like many of the popular R&B artist who name the name of Christ having only a form of godliness but denying the power thereof.

At a time in my life when I felt I needed more money, I resigned from the church and started playing in a dance hall; a great jump from $2.50 per week to $7.50 per night, plus tips, one meal, and transportation. Before too long the pastor and superintendent and deacons told me that a Christian should trust God to take care of him or her and should not be in a dance hall or joint. I knew I was not satisfied in the dance hall so, I returned to my post as pianist/organist, being definitely sorry for having strayed away. From that day to this, God has positively and bountifully taken care of my loved ones and me.

My first child I gave back to God when she was one month old. I still remember what a beautiful Christian she was. My second child, a girl, lived only two weeks and one day. My first husband died and the children of my second marriage (a girl and a boy) were each given back to God when they were one month old. My first child and my husband were baptized during the same service at our church. Lawrence Weeden and I enjoyed our lives together in our church and service to the Lord until his death in 1977. My youngest daughter and my son were baptized during the same service at our church. My daughter is a very dedicated Christian and active in her local church. My son, a Vietnam veteran, has strayed away from the things of God. But when I remember the time when they both sought Christ, I definitely feel God will bring him back into full commitment to the Lord before too long. This is my daily prayer.

So many men were not only physically wounded but psychologically, mentally, and spiritually wounded. He contracted Asian Orange [sic] and I had to watch him suffer the ill effects of this war. Flashbacks occurred frequently. I could hear him re-living war scenes in his back bedroom. He became more and more despondent. His physical appearance was unkempt. What happened to my handsome, once strong and happy son? He had periods of anger and fits of violence.

Had this same God who had gifted me with the ability of music and had given me the desire to serve Him through church ministry, all these 80 years abandon me? Why, hadn't I often played the hymn, "No Never Alone, He promised never to leave me, no never alone" I continued to emerse my son in prayer. Daily for years I would stand in my church prayer meeting and place his name on the request list.

My house was old. I had lived in it for over 40 years. It was placed on the condemned list. I was moved to a senior citizen high rise on Mohammed Ali Boulevard. What was to become of my son, we all so affectionately called, Sonny? He was placed in a veteran's hospital.

"You have a visitor" was the message I received from the front desk attendant. There standing cleaned, shaved, and in a repaired mind, stood my own prodigal, not lured away by riches and rebellion but by the evil effects of a war zone. He was back! I had no fatted lambs to kill or any feast to spread. I was only a mother with a small widow's pension. However, I could shower him with the blessings of praise to God who had not forsaken me.

I have other loved ones that I feel in my heart are dedicated, born again Christians. For this I am so very grateful. In my loneliest hour, my God and my church are always near to comfort and to guide me. I thank the almighty God for all these blessings!

"The days of our years are threescore years and ten; and if by reason of strength they be fourscore years, yet is their strength, labor and sorrow, for it is soon cut off, and we fly away." Psalm 90:10.

What examples seniors can play in the master symphony of God's plan. I praise God for many senior examples in the church who are living fulfilled godly lives. They are not griping and complaining and just sitting around watching television or vegetating, but truly are encouragers, giving us younger women admonishing from the Lord. They are found praying without ceasing and having a glow that says, the longer I serve Him, the sweeter He grows.

I praise the Lord for this particular senior because she is my grandmother. She writes me often on a slip of paper with a heading which reads: "My God Isn't Dead, I Talked To Him This Morning." She has outlived most of her relatives. She's also lived long enough to see her prayer answered, the son, the Vietnam vet, return to an abundant life in Christ. He is the one she can count on to spoon feed her because arthritis causes her to shake so until the food falls off the utensil. He is the one who is there to help her with a variety of personal tasks, even returning the letters written to her great-grandchildren.

It is with utmost confidence that even as I write these lines, my grandmother, old and feeble in body, is young and strong in faith. She prays for me daily. Missions and the spread of the gospel was very important to her. For years, on her lowly pension, and dreams of her "ship" coming in where she could afford to give in abundance, she gave to the work of the Lord at home and abroad. On my mission field in South Africa, I could lay my head to rest each night knowing my grandmother prayed without ceasing for me.

FOR DISCUSSION

#1   One of the greatest inheritances we receive from our elderly relatives is the wealth of their experiences.

Recall an incident told to you by one of your elderly relatives.

#2 Increasingly, adult health and day care are real concerns for our elderly relatives. What facilities are available in your area? Would you be happy living or having to attend these facilities?

#3 How can seniors guard against becoming old and bitter as so many are accused of being these days?

#4 How can those in the younger generation assist in making the sunset years of our aged loved ones beautiful?

#5 How can we practically obey the 5th commandment "honor thy mother and thy father"?

Chapter Four

Chapter Four
REMEMBERING THE 60s

by Roberta Dowdy

I survived the sixties! Those extremely difficult years for me as a woman, wife, mother, and black. My physical life began in Arkansas but my awareness began in Benton Harbor, Michigan in a transient, well established suburb of both Detroit and Chicago. A transient town because hundreds of Blacks poured in yearly for fruit harvest, established because those few Blacks who had been there 20-50 years were entrenched in their private life styles and disassociated from much of the seething turmoil that is still to be found there.

Those never-to-be forgotten Sixties! They were life-changing for not only me, my husband and children, but for the entire world. There was not one person nor family that wasn't affected by the events of that decade. To highlight some of the main happenings, let me run down the years quickly:

1960--Non-violent sit-ins began in cafeterias, libraries, beaches, Woolworth's. Birth control pills were okayed for general use.

1961--Bay of Pigs Disaster; 23rd Amendment passed, giving D.C. residents the right to vote in national elections. Green Berets were ordered to Vietnam. Alan B. Shepard, Jr. spends 15 min. in space.

1962--Prayer was taken from public schools. Thalidomide banned in US after causing birth defects in Europe. Marilyn Monroe dies!

1963--University of Mississippi was integrated by James Meredith. Medgar Evers, civil rights leader was killed. MLK, Jr. was jailed in Alabama. The Civil Rights March in Washington took place, King's "I Have A Dream" speech was delivered. Betty Friedan writes *Feminine Mystic*. President JF Kennedy was assassinated.

1964--Civil Rights Bill signed into law by President LB Johnson Three Civil Rights workers were slain in Mississippi. Race riots broke out in New York.

1965--Vietnam War caused more US troops to be sent. Malcolm X was assassinated. Watts went up in flames.

1966--Supreme Court outlawed Poll Tax for all Federal elections, allowing Blacks to vote in the South. Federal funds for birth control were legalized. Anti-war protests divided the nation. More race riots in Atlanta and Chicago.

1967--Detroit race riot recorded as worst in US history. Head of Defense resigns.

1968--Martin Luther King, Jr. assassinated. Robert Kennedy assassinated. Black protest seen at Olympics.

1969--Supreme Court orders school desegregation for all schools. Neil Armstrong walks on the Moon. Drugs and sex abuse, protest, and cult movements are on the rise.

Although in 1954, the Supreme Court had already ordered desegregation for all schools in the South. That law became the snowball that began rolling through the years, finally colliding with white values, life-styles, and traditions, causing an explosion felt around the world.

We, as a family, had taught our children to respect all peoples. We knew from personal experience, that we had to "prove" ourselves; college years and job seeking had taught us, very well, that lesson, often, the hard way! We had doors slammed; resumes ignored, entrance denied, rejected applications, housing refused, and services withheld. All of these things hurt us, but we tried not to become bitter, or filled with hatred as did so many. But it is really hard when your own children are physically hurt because of the color God has given them. It was then realized that I truly needed more than I had to help them, to help support my husband in his struggles on the job that he had to fight for to attain and gain any recognition. God used those trials and the Sixties to get my attention. In His sovereignty I survived the sixties. Those were extremely difficult years for me.

The sixties found me married, mother of five, and a part-time professional. I felt disillusioned, empty, guilt-ridden, lonely, depressed, and fearful. Having mere "religion" as my foundation, when the uproar of the races was being heard, seen, as well as felt, the shabby make-shift base upon which I so desperately tried to stand seemed to wobble. I felt like it veered crazily off the course I desired to follow, thus filling me with all those feelings. Empty--at a time of life when days were filled, scheduled in advance, busy! Responsibilities were at their peak with all five children in school and three of them teenagers. As a mother I felt my duty was to be actively involved in their education so I served diligently at three schools, available for whatever, whenever, wherever. In addition to the participation with our children, I was active for personal fulfillment in no less than three social clubs. Although one was a service group for the elderly of our Black community, none of these was church-based or Christian-oriented. There were also various functions for my husband that were a part of my busy schedule, yet deep within was a void, an emptiness unexplained, something was missing.

My guilt feelings, which I hid very well even from myself, would surface in the form of depression. There would be days when the mood would be heavy, almost unbearable, but at no time was suicide planned. To run away, leave all, to begin again, yes! These were in my thoughts quite often. The end results of such moods would be deeper involvement with a group or to seek even newer activities in which to lose myself. Loneliness was a constant companion even in my large family. With all the activities, associates, and co-workers, I was one who was lonely in a crowd. There seemed to be no one I felt would understand the inner feelings I needed desperately to share. There had been my mother--a strong submissive Christian. Just to spend time with her was always a release for me, but she died just before the sixties (October '59). That was the greatest loss of my life.

Fear didn't plague me until the racial unrest and moral decline of our society became so prevalent. The three older children were ripe for both areas and my concerns turned to fear when I realized no foundation had been lain for self knowledge and guiding principles. What was to become of them, their tender lives, their future? I felt helpless. To whom could I turn for aid, for answers, for strength to go on? It was while in the midst of these turbulent times that an old acquaintance met me in front of a store. She greeted me warmly, sincerely inquiring about the family and the events in each life. Then as we were parting she handed me a leaflet. Now this was the very first time I can remember receiving a gospel tract. To this day I have not read it, but the title convicted my heart, "The Age of Accountability," on the cover, the face of a child. A new felt pang of guilt took over--parental neglect. What had I taught the children about God? Were they past the age of accountability? My friend's parting words were, "I'm praying for you!"

How often I have praised the Lord for those words and her precious ministry in my life during the months that followed. That encounter plus other events caused me to search for spiritual answers. I began to read my Bible, at random, to talk with church members, even listen to radio sermons on Sundays. I was seeking some direction for my life, desperate to salvage mine and my family's.

Another friend was used by the Lord to invite me to a ladies' retreat. Three days and nights away from confusion and noise. Days filled with Bible teaching and the love of God being bountifully manifested in every action of those responsible for the retreat workshops. It was then in comparison by stark contrast, I saw myself, my greatest need--to respond to the love of God, through Jesus Christ, His son who loved me and gave Himself for my sins. As the Holy Spirit convicted me, wooing me into submission, I yielded my rights to my life, giving myself over to receive Jesus Christ as Savior.

Even now as I recall that August night 1970, my heart overflows! Such love, such greater love, that special love that Christ had for me, even before my conception, even while I snubbed Him, mocked Him in my attempts at religion, He loved me. How precious that knowledge is to me. It is my assurance for He loves me still and shows me daily. I gave my heart to Jesus on August 18, 1970 to be my Savior, and, on January 4, 1972, I yielded my life, total commitment, allowing Him to become Lord of my life.

Following my salvation, I became so hungry for His word. I devoured the scriptures. First the New Testament, then the Old. I became involved in a home Bible study class with two dear friends in our home and four of our children within six weeks were members of God's true family. My husband also received Christ as his saviour. How I thank God for all the many people He has allowed in my life for they have either encouraged, challenged, taught me, been a source of strength to me, or just a companion in Christ, shouldering burdens with me. Even for my enemies who have taught me lessons, God allowed me to learn through them. Till He comes or calls for me, I desire to be steadfast, unmovable, always abounding in the work of the Lord, knowing that my efforts are not in vain in Him!

I love sharing the Word of God with all who desire to hear, especially women. We hold the very heart strings of our society in our hands, shaping and molding our future. Our ignorance of God's design, plans, and purposes for the family is sadly being manifested in every aspect of our lives. It is seen in our homes, prevalent in our churches, and spilling--no--flooding our social structure, and undermining its foundations.

We as Blacks have just been taken back to our "roots," but we didn't go back far enough. Adam's sin nature became ours by birth. Christ commands us to be born again in order to see the Kingdom as well as enter it. Take heed to His call, Matthew 11:28-30, accept His love, grow in His Grace, become His ambassador.

I am eternally grateful for many ambassadors who endeavored to improve race relations and civil unrest; Andrew Young, Rosa Parks, Shirley Chisholm, Dr. Martin L. King, Jr., and others. God is and has always been very concerned with race relations and civil rights. For every age He has always sent a "Moses." At the same time, He reminds us in His word, that everyone of us shall give an account of himself to God. "For we must all appear before the judgment seat of Christ; that everyone may receive the things done in his body, according to that he hath done, whether it be good or bad" (II Corinthians 5:10).

Governments, city officials, employees, and civilians alike will have to give an account for the very decisions which were made unjustly. Klu Klux Klan members, who burned, raped, and stripped blacks of their very dignity will have to give an account to a Holy and Just Judge of the universe. Likewise, because God said, "Vengeance is mine..." (Psalm 94), we, as victims will be held responsible for how we respond. How we free ourselves from bitterness, retaliation, anger, and even self rejection is even more important. What do we tell our children? Have we really released ourselves from the nightmares of the 60s? Are many of the chains of slavery bound to our very souls even here in the 90s?

The gospel record of John so boldly tells us, "If the Son therefore shall make you free, ye shall be free indeed." May the truth of this scripture be a reality in your life. I have so much to praise God and my Lord Jesus for!!! Truly, He has delivered me from the powers of darkness.

"We wrestle not against flesh and blood, but against principalities, against powers, against the rulers of the darkness of this world, against spiritual wickedness in high places. Wherefore, take unto you the whole armor of God, that ye may be able to withstand in the evil day, and having done all to stand." Ephesians 6:12-13

Much has been said regarding just how far we have or have not advanced from the 60s with regards to racial relations, morality, and women's rights. Significant progress has been made in reducing racial segregation. Yet despite the gains of nearly thirty years, the festering sores of poverty, racism, and violence continue to frustrate hope. We can rejoice in the fact that in the sixties we had fewer than 100 Black-elected officials and today there are over 7,000 Black office holders. We have a lot more freedoms, but liberty and justice remain scarce. In many instances, there is greater tolerance, greater respect, greater recognition of the fact that we must find ways to live together, to work together, to worship together, because the only alternative is to suffer and/or die together.

The Christian African-American woman cannot afford to retrieve and become complacent to the battles of segregation, poverty, job discrimination, race rioting, low education standards, and, worse of all, Black-on-Black violence. One way this can be done is by becoming a part like what I recently saw in a Detroit community where women held all night prayer vigils to take back their neighborhoods from gangs, drugs, and despair. Things happen when women pray.

Mothers have to become involved in the schools where our children attend. One of the saddest sights I saw while teaching eight years of secondary education was the scene at parent-teacher conferences where less than ten percent of the Black parents showed up. There are MOMS IN TOUCH prayer and support groups that are making a difference in the communities where these support groups exist. Increasingly, the body of Jesus Christ, members of local churches, have had to voice protest and concerns for human rights. Tolerance and 'window-dressing of integrated race relations will not do. Even now as we begin to worship together, we should say as the Psalmist..."Lord, try my heart and see if there be any wicked way in me" (Psalm 139: 23-24). We can barely fool our neighbor let alone God. As black and white Christians, if the world can not see the love of Jesus in us, in whom will they see it? Our homes need our involvement. Our churches and our communities need us now in the 90s even more than we were needed in the 60s. The war has already been won through our Lord Jesus Christ, but the battle is not over.

DISCUSSION QUESTIONS

#1   What human right issues of today should the Church of Jesus Christ be concerned with?

#2   Could you agree with these statements? Christians need to take a united stand against corruption that is taking place in our land. For evil to triumph, good men and women should do nothing.

#3   Can you recall a personal unjust experience which happened to you or a family member? How do you handle the emotions that arise?

#4   What would be your first response if your child came home and told you his/her choice for a life partner was of another race?

#5   Can one ever forget the past? What do we learn from the past to better our future?

Reflections of Christian Women

Chapter Five

Chapter Five
A MINISTER'S WIFE

by H. Susie Ezell

Forty years ago, the Lord laid a burden upon the hearts of two single American ladies to be missionaries to Morocco (North Africa). Morocco is primarily a Muslim country. Alice and Beth (not their real names, American missionaries can be targeted for persecution by Muslims then as well as today) went as they were led by the Lord to work in the midst of the people in a little town called Azrou.

Most Moroccans are descended from Berbers or from Arabs who invaded the country during the Muslin conquest. There are also twenty-thousand Jews living in Morocco, plus an ever-changing small population of black nomads called the Hauatines, who are a desert tribe. The population of Morocco is over twenty million. Arabic is spoken in the cities and along the seacoasts, with Berber still the native language in the remote districts. Almost all Moroccans can speak several languages. French and Spanish are easily understood by most people in the cities.

The Berber life-style centers around the tribe. Everyone in a tribe can trace his/her family back to a common ancestor. There are at least six hundred different Berber tribes. Alice and Beth were happy serving the Lord there. One day they heard a knock at the door. There standing in the doorway was a young woman and a small bundle. The young woman asked them to please take her bundle. Somehow they were not amazed that the bundle was a baby, but told the young woman they had not come to Morocco to take in children but to work and intermingle among the people and tell them about Christ.

After the young mother left with her baby, the Lord began speaking to their hearts, telling them what greater way could they lead ones to Christ but to bring them up as children? Statistics show that one percent of individuals who receive Christ as Saviour do so by the age of four. Eighty-five percent of individuals who receive Christ as Saviour do so between the ages of 4-14. Ten percent are saved between the ages of 14-30.

Only five percent who receive Christ as Saviour do so past the age of thirty.

So they prayed to the Lord and asked Him if this were His desire for their lives. If this is how God wanted to use them, they were willing, and He would send them the children. Sure enough, a baby boy (Fred) was brought to them. As he grew older, they prayed that God would send him a brother. Not too long after this request, the Lord sent him a sister. As word began spreading about these two American missionary ladies taking in unwanted children, the home began to grow and grow. I was the sixth child to arrive at the home.

The Children's Haven in Morocco is a faith mission. The support to care for the home comes from the missionaries and their supporting churches in the United States. Some of the children have individual sponsors from the states, but primary support comes from the missionaries for all running expenses.

During my twenty years at the home, the support had to care for about hundred people. This included all the Moroccan children plus the missionaries and their children. We had no government help. Not one day passed that we went without a meal. At times when funds were low, we would pray and see how God would answer our prayers. Maybe the next day a check would be in the mail, or someone may come to visit and would leave us a gift of money. The Lord always provided.

The clothes and shoes we wore were received from friends, and some of our clothes were handmade. We seldom received anything new, but the things we received were in good condition and we were grateful. The home is located on five acres of land. We had several large buildings. In the main building was where most of the activities took place such as in the large kitchen, dinning room, and living room. We had our own chapel where we met every Sunday for worship services. Two services were held. Sunday mornings, the service was preached in the native Arabic tongue. The other service was preached in English.

Most visitors who would come and visit would say the home reminded them of camp. We would rise each day at 6:00AM.

Only five percent who receive Christ as Saviour do so past the age of thirty.

So they prayed to the Lord and asked Him if this were His desire for their lives. If this is how God wanted to use them, they were willing, and He would send them the children. Sure enough, a baby boy (Fred) was brought to them. As he grew older, they prayed that God would send him a brother. Not too long after this request, the Lord sent him a sister. As word began spreading about these two American missionary ladies taking in unwanted children, the home began to grow and grow. I was the sixth child to arrive at the home.

The Children's Haven in Morocco is a faith mission. The support to care for the home comes from the missionaries and their supporting churches in the United States. Some of the children have individual sponsors from the states, but primary support comes from the missionaries for all running expenses.

During my twenty years at the home, the support had to care for about hundred people. This included all the Moroccan children plus the missionaries and their children. We had no government help. Not one day passed that we went without a meal. At times when funds were low, we would pray and see how God would answer our prayers. Maybe the next day a check would be in the mail, or someone may come to visit and would leave us a gift of money. The Lord always provided.

The clothes and shoes we wore were received from friends, and some of our clothes were handmade. We seldom received anything new, but the things we received were in good condition and we were grateful. The home is located on five acres of land. We had several large buildings. In the main building was where most of the activities took place such as in the large kitchen, dining room, and living room. We had our own chapel where we met every Sunday for worship services. Two services were held. Sunday mornings, the service was preached in the native Arabic tongue. The other service was preached in English.

Most visitors who would come and visit would say the home reminded them of camp. We would rise each day at 6:00AM.

Breakfast was served at 7:00 AM. We completed our chores before going to school (which was also located on the premises). The missionaries were our teachers. School began at 8:00AM. At noon we broke for lunch and continued with our chores. We returned to school which usually ended by 4:00PM. Supper was served at 5:00. We did our chores and our homework. Bedtime varied according to age.

Each week day was filled with scheduled activities, such as Mon--staff business, Tue--free time, Wed--prayer meeting, Thurs--mother and father evening where the girls would get together and chat with our "moms" and the boys would get together and chat with the men (fathers). Fri- was fun night where together we would play games and have refreshments. Saturday night we had vespers where we would get together and sing, have special music and, then, a story related to Biblical truths.

The home is still in existence today but with fewer children. The missionaries are growing old in age and not as able to take in more children. Many children offered to them have been turned away to other government agencies. Please pray that God's work will continue. Younger missionary couples are needed to take care of the babies and children in the haven and bring them up under the guidance of the Lord.

When those of us who were there from the beginning graduated from high school, we had a choice to either continue education in college or find work. Many of my original family left the home, found work, married, or even came to the States to college. We are scattered all over the world. Praise the Lord for the missionaries (my family). If it were not for them, where would I be today?

My biological mother had recently gone through a divorce and was unable to raise me alone. She knew of some nuns who took in children until a certain age where they would then turn over to government care. My mother, then eight months pregnant, asked the nuns if they would take her child when it was born. They weren't able to take another newborn, but they told her there were two American missionaries who could. My mother walked further down the road until she came to their home.

She told them of her dilemma and asked if they would take her child when it was born. They were happy to do so. In fact, my mother stayed in their home until I was born and then returned to her village. I know while in their home my mother had opportunity to hear about the Lord and to this day I continue to pray for her salvation.

Being accepted into this home was the beginning of God's sovereign hand of mercy on me. He chose me out of all the many, many unwanted children to be born and placed in a home called The Children's Haven. There I learned day by day about Christ. However, it wasn't until I was twelve years-old that I personally asked Jesus into my heart. I had seen the routine of receiving Christ because many of my older brothers and sisters in the home had given their lives to Jesus; I thought I could mimic what they did too. So many people are just that way, mimicking the Christian life; there is no real genuineness of new birth.

In 1968, we had an earthquake in our country. I was asleep on the top bunk, and I awoke to the trembling. Everything was shaking. I asked my sister, if this room caved in were we ready to go to Heaven? By my being on the top bunk, I just knew I'd be the first to die. I was scared and at the same time joking just a little. The earthquake subsided, but the trembling in my soul continued. Even at the age of twelve, I was under conviction by the Holy Spirit. Was I ready to meet the Saviour if I should die? That Sunday evening March 1968, I knocked on one of my mother's doors; I told her that I wanted to ask Jesus into my heart. She was so excited. Even though it was midnight, I couldn't sleep. She opened her Bible and read some salvation scriptures to me. One verse that stands out so vividly in my mind is Revelation 3:20 "Behold I stand at the door and knock; if any man hear my voice and open the door, I will come in to him and will sup with him and he with me."

Even though Satan was doing his best to keep me from leaving my bed and going to my mothers to have them lead me to the Lord, I refused to listen. I had often heard the promise of the word of God, that He so loved the world, that He gave His only begotten son that whosoever believeth on Him should not perish but have everlasting life (John 3:16). I am His child forever! "I give unto them eternal life, and they shall never perish, neither shall any man pluck them out of my hand" (John 10:28). When I gave my life to Jesus, I knew at that moment that I belonged to Him and that my life was His to lead as He pleased. I wanted to serve Him totally. I knew He wanted me in full time Christian service. I dreamed of marrying a minister.

At age nineteen, I graduated from high school. The Lord was leading me to attend Bible school. I began to pray for the Lord's guidance as to what school to attend. I applied to several Bible schools but had not received a reply from any of them. One day while thumbing through the pages of the Moody Monthly, I saw a small advertisement of Carver Bible College in Atlanta, GA. The bold print read, **Training Black Men and Women for the Ministry.** I knew within my heart everything was going to work out because this was God's will. "For we know all things work together for good to them that are called according to His purpose" (Romans 8:28-31). I had peace within. Obtaining my passport which is usually a long drawn out process, I received in one week! I applied to Carver and was accepted. I was told I could work in the cafeteria to help pay my tuition.

In July of 1977, I flew to the U.S.A. to attend Carver Bible College. My initial intentions upon graduation, I felt, was to return to the Children's Haven to help bring up other children in the Saving Knowledge of my Lord and Saviour Jesus Christ. The Lord even allowed me to be able to save enough money to return to Morocco for the summer and work at the home. After a summer of working in the home, I returned to Carver. God made it clear that He had something else for my life. "I shall give you the desires of your heart" (Psalm 37:4).

In the early 1940s, the Paynes were burdened to help Black pastors learn the Bible. In the fall of 1943, Carver Bible Institute began. The Paynes named the school after Dr. George Washington Carver, the renowned Black Christian and scientist. The first classes were held in a store front facility acquired on Chestnut Street in Atlanta, Georgia. The hunger of Black students for the Word of God was confirmed, and the school grew beyond the capacity of the Chestnut facility. Having sought the Lord's leading for additional space for growth, the Paynes relocated the school in Southwest Atlanta. Dr. Payne labored with Carver Bible College until his death. Dr. William Hungerpiller became president where he served for many years.

Carver Bible College is basically structured to prepare men and women for full time Christian work. Subjects are Biblical courses but other courses are offered as well. Two types of degrees are offered. Bachelors in Biblical Education, if you take Greek and pass! Or a Bachelor of Arts equivalent to an Associates two-year degree. I would highly recommend Carver Bible College if you are led of the Lord into full time ministry. Even for part time study, Carver Bible College is a great place to learn the word of God and become more equipped to serve Him anywhere. And what about my dream of marrying a minister?

God brought a young man into my life who was also attending Carver. He was preparing for the pastorate. I graduated in 1981 with a Bachelors in Biblical Education. Tim had a year to go, so I moved to his hometown in Michigan and began working and making plans for our wedding. He graduated in May 1982, and we were married that June. Tim served as an associate pastor for about five years. He also served as an interim pastor for about two years. In 1986, the Lord laid it upon our hearts and opened the doors for the awesome opportunity and challenge of full time pastoring at Mt. Calvary Christian Bible Church. We started with just four members and the Lord has continued to build His church and currently we have nearly 150 members including children.

Dreams and desires come true, but they are also accompanied with trials and hard roads and obstacles. The Lord has been with us always and is bringing us through. I am proud of what God is doing through my husband. Our missionary contributions include supporting the Children's Haven still in Morocco. I grew up having to help raise 30 of my own brothers and sisters in the Children's Haven. This has helped me greatly in my service at Mt. Calvary Christian Bible Church.

I have an opportunity to meet with a group of ministers' wives the second Monday of the month for fellowship and encouragement. I serve as the chaplain. There are ministers' wives of all different denominations. We've studied several books, one entitled, *Becoming the Noble Woman*. There is so much work to do.

A verse that has meant so much to me during my Christian walk is Proverbs 3:5-6: "Trust in the Lord with all thine heart and lean not unto thy own understanding, in all thy ways acknowledge Him and He shall direct thy paths." I have trusted Him all these years to plan my life for me. In 1984, the Lord blessed Tim and me with a son, and, then, He chose to take him home to be with Him several hours after birth. This loss was very painful for us, but we've been comforted with the verse in II Samuel 12:22-23, where David cried to the Lord that his child would live, but God chose to take him to glory. David said, I shall go to him, but he shall not return to me. We know that one day when the rapture comes we will see our son, Malcolm. In 1985 we were blessed with our first daughter Jamela Marie, and in 1986 we were blessed with a second daughter, Christina.

I have so much to be thankful for as I look back over my thirty-something years of life. God snatched me out of a Moslem home and placed me in a God fearing Christian Children's Haven where I could come to know Him personally. He allowed me the opportunity to attend Bible school and gave me a wonderful, sincere Christian husband and children and extended church family. God is with us leading and guiding our lives and promised never to leave us. Praise Him for all His goodness, kindness, and mercies which shall follow us (Tim, Susie, Jamela, Christina) all the days of our lives, and one day we will dwell in the house of the Lord forever. Praise His wonderful name!

Daily works from morn' till night, perfect children, act just right, house is always neat and clean, company may soon be seen. Cheerfully at every meeting, smiling nicely with her greeting. Slim, trim, and always fit confident and quick with wit.

Thrifty, smart, and pretty, too, knows the Bible through and through. Cooks and entertains with zest, never worried, never stressed. Talent, charm, and patient too, nothing that she cannot do. Never existing in real life, she's the mythical preacher's wife!

by Carolyn Simpson, a pastor's wife in Mobile, Alabama

The call of being a wife is awesome. Imagine the call of being a minister's wife. I have witnessed one too many local churches having to suffer from the consequences of divorce as it hits the Christian community and robs us of our testimonies and thriving ministries. One too many churches has been robbed of their effectiveness because of the testimonies of the pastor and his wife. Today more than ever the church, the world needs the ministry of spirit filled by ministers' wives. As the poem states, there are many unrealistic expectations that people thrust upon ministers' wives, and, yet at the same time, ministers' wives roles are not that they sit modestly dressed, dawned in their best "Sunday go to meeting hat."

The minister's wife has a key role to play, and God needs her there. There is one vivid example I remember most from my pastor's wife. Vivian always stood by her husband's side at the door following Sunday services. She also exemplified the oneness of their ministry in numerous ways. She never openly or publicly criticized her husband/pastor. She gave love, hope, and strength for the ministry they share together.

The minister **needs** his wife. He needs a creatively giving spiritual, emotional, and practical help mate, who will add a unique and vibrant dimension that permeates an entire church fellowship and brings completeness to its ministry. The minister's wife should complement the husband's leadership, which cannot function well without this dual quality. Together they can embody traits and skills, which by the way, come more naturally to women than to men. Leadership is more closely akin to nurturing than to ruling, more like guiding than demanding, more like serving than being served. The minister's wife who combines the qualities of selflessness with the qualities of a shared vision, passion, commitment, and encourager becomes part of a team (church body) that can't be beat.

This is a tall order, you say. Yes, I agree. Yet like the Lord told Zerubbabel, He tells us, "Not by might, nor by power, but by my spirit" Zechariah 4:6. Other practical tips include making sure you say something daily to build your husband/pastor. Have consistent personal devotions. Deepen your prayer life by keeping a prayer journal. Prayer journals often include a daily devotional scripture text. Pages are provided for one to write out specific daily prayer request.

Sample:

Mondays:	Missionaries or church missions supported by your church
Tuesdays:	Tasks the wife/husband or other family members need to complete
Wednesdays:	Wants and needs
Thursdays:	Page filled with thanksgiving
Fridays:	Family and friends
Saturdays:	Sunday services
Sundays:	Specific prayer for salvation needs or church supporters

Learn to be comfortable with women of all ages, young, middle-aged, and elderly, women with peaceful spirits, generous hearts, and a good sense of humor. Pray for, but avoid becoming close to women who are angry, contentious, habitual complainers, or fault finders. Encouraging ministers' wives support groups are great, but be sure they are groups which are truly seeking the kingdom of God. Be careful to guard support groups from becoming complaint centers or centers for ministry comparisons. One pastor's wives group meets once a month beginning with a devotional challenge, a time of testimony, has a planned ministry for a collective local need--where the community can see the church of God working together rather that as elite groups on different corners comparing one another. Each session closes in prayers of encouragement for one another in ministry.

I don't want to end this section without mentioning the importance of those of us in the pews to enrapture the truth of 1 Corinthians 3:9a, "For we are laborers together with God." We need the minister's wife, and she needs us.

FOR DISCUSSION:

#1   If you are in full time Christian ministry either as a pastor's wife, para-church organization, missionary, evangelist. etc. what do you request most often as prayer concerns?

#2   According to I Timothy chapter 3 list the qualities which would be of real necessity for women in positions of a called ministry.

#3   How can a pastor's wife's faith really be challenged in situations when her husband/pastor is in the wrong or the church is in conflict?

#4   What are some ways pastor's wives deal with the fact that their husbands' and family times are always in demand?

#5   Recently, how have you shown appreciation to the pastor's wife?

Chapter Six

Chapter Six
A MISSIONARY FOR THE LORD

by Beverly Frowner

Yes, I am a Christian African-American woman and thank God for how He has wonderfully made me for His glory. I am one of nine children born to Alex and Hazel Johnson. My mother told me an elderly saint had wanted to name me Beverly. She and Mama prayed for me before I was born. Praise the Lord for praying Black Christian women. I was born on February 17, 1941, in Chicago, Illinois. Mama prayed for our family everyday of her life for which I am very thankful. Her prayers were to see the whole family walk with the Lord. She took us to Sunday school, church, afternoon programs and evening services. She told us about God and Jesus Christ, and we were without excuse for not being saved (Romans 1).

From the time I entered this world, God has been speaking to my heart as He speaks to everyone. I learned John 3:16 and knew it well in my head, all my heart needed to do was to believe it. I did at the age of 8. I was not looking for God. He was looking for me and found me. John 15:16 is my life verse, "Ye have not chosen me, but I have chosen you, and ordained you that ye should go and bring forth fruit, and that your fruit should remain: that whatsoever ye shall ask of the Father in my name, He may give it you." Because I know that God so loved the world, that He gave His only begotten Son, that whosoever believeth in Him should not perish, but have everlasting life, I asked Jesus Christ to come into my heart that I might go to heaven to live with Him forever, which is a fact.

I base my life on facts not feelings. I might feel saved today and lost the next, but God's word tells me I am saved forever. John 3:36, "He that believeth on the Son hath everlasting life; and he that believeth not the Son shall not see life; but the wrath of God abideth on him."

1 John 5:23, "These things have I written unto you that believe on the name of the Son of God that ye may know that ye have eternal life, and that ye may believe on the name of the Son of God." John 20:31, "But these are written, that ye might believe that Jesus is the Christ, the Son of God; and that believing ye might have life through His name." Yes, I know that I am going to heaven. No guessing, hoping, thinking, or wishing -- God's word tells me so I believe it.

At the age of 16, I went to a Christian camp and learned how to serve the Lord. The fellowship was great. It was a mixed group, black and white Christians working together for God's glory. I dedicated my life to serve the Lord that year. I couldn't understand why God had chosen me to have such a rich and wonderful time at camp. I wanted everyone to be there, too. But this was the leading of the Holy Spirit in my life and I said yes to the Lord. Here at this camp I learned about temperance and total abstinence from alcoholic beverages. We saw a movie on how beer was made, and it was a sorrowful sight. Remembering the sights I saw on the streets of Chicago and the ugly effects of alcohol made a great impression on my life not to touch it. We saw a movie on smoking as well, and I purposed in my heart like Daniel in the Bible not to smoke or drink.

In my early teen years, I heard an African-American missionary woman who had been in Africa for a number of years serving the Lord. She told us how the Africans wanted to know why they didn't have more Black missionaries to tell them about Jesus. She told us to pray for Christian mates while we were young. I did just that and prayed that I would marry a Christian man, and not just a Christian man but one who was committed and on fire for God.

After high school, I went to junior college for two years. I started well, but finished badly. As far as I was concerned that was the end of school. Then I met a beautiful African-American Christian young lady by the name of Evelyn. The beauty was in her Christian character. You could see Jesus in her life. She was working for Illinois Bell Telephone, and I was working for Newmode Hosiery Co. Our jobs were walking distance from each other. Evelyn was attending Moody Bible Institute and asked me to go the next term. I didn't want to hear anything about going to school so I told her no. She kept after me until finally I decided to give it a try. This again was the leading of the Holy Spirit in my life.

I started at Moody and fell in love with school. I purposed in my heart to go and learn all I could about God, His Son, the Lord Jesus Christ. The word of God is rich, and it will change your life. I had no desire to graduate when I started. I just wanted to learn how to be a better Christian African-American woman and be used by God for His service. In 1971 I graduated from Moody Bible Institute Evening School. Praise the Lord!

The summer before I started Moody, I met another fine Christian, Webster Carver Frowner. He is both fine in looks and character, a perfect gentleman. We met on a church picnic, and I invited him to go to Moody with me that fall. Webster went to Moody for a semester and then joined the United States Army. I was working days and going to school evenings.

Webster wanted to get married, and I felt I wasn't ready for marriage. My family loved him and my friends loved him, too. While attending Moody I went to a meeting called Operation Mobilization. From this group students would go to Canada, Mexico, and Europe to do tract and book ministry. The Holy Spirit was speaking to my heart to go. I prayed about it, and with a girlfriend, Phylis Kay, we went to Belgium and France for a summer. I asked God to see one soul come into His family and He answered that prayer. Praised the Lord!

While I was in France, Webster (now my fiancé) was in Germany waiting to meet me there. I knew the Lord was leading me into holy matrimony. We both had prayed while apart that God's will be done in our lives as husband and wife. I then knew that my high calling would be to be a Christian wife and mother. I knew my responsibilities to God, my husband and children. So many today do not consider this a HIGH calling.

My husband--

"And the Lord God caused a deep sleep to fall upon Adam and he slept. And He took one of his ribs and closed up the flesh instead thereof; And the rib, which the Lord God had taken from man, made He woman, and brought her unto the man. And Adam said, this is now bone of my bones, and flesh of my flesh and she shall be called woman, because she was taken out of man. Therefore, shall man leave his father and mother and shall cleave unto his wife; and they shall be one flesh and they were both naked, the man and his wife, and were not ashamed" (Genesis 2:21-25).

"Unto the woman He said, I will greatly multiply thy sorrow and thy conception; in sorrow thou shalt bring forth children; and thy desire shall be to thy husband, and he shall rule over thee" (Genesis 3:16).

"Wives, submit yourselves unto your own husband, as unto the Lord" (Ephesians 5:22).

"Wives, submit yourselves unto your own husbands, as it is fit in the Lord" (Colossians 3:18).

"Likewise, ye wives, be in subjection to your own husbands; if any obey not the word, they also may without the word be won by the conversations of the wives" (I Peter 3:1).

My heart's cry is that Christian African-American women let the men be head of the home. We know this can only come about by the working of the Holy Spirit in our lives . We can't do it, but He can!

My Children--

"Train up a child in the way he should go; and when he is old, he will not depart from it" (Proverbs 6:22).

"Children, obey your parents in all things; for this is well pleasing unto the Lord" (Colossians 3:20).

Today we can not afford to let children train themselves or be trained by ungodly educators. The responsibility is ours. I will have to give an answer at the Bema (the Judgment Seat of Christ) for how I have lived as a Christian woman, wife, and mother.

Webster came to France and worked with the boy's team and I with the girl's team in witnessing in France. He stayed two weeks, and we both went back to Germany. We wanted Christ to be the head of our home and lives. On September 10 and 11 we were married--first by the German counselor and on the next day by the United States Army chaplain.

We spent fifteen months in Germany, and God taught us many lessons as we started our lives together as Mr. & Mrs. Webster Carver Frowner. Don't think we didn't have our problems. We did, but we let the Lord work them out. We had our first child in Germany, a son, David Webster. We returned home to the USA and made Chicago our home. Webster went back to Moody and graduated. He pastored the West Pullman Baptist Church. We have four wonderful children.

I met the author of this book's mother, who is now present with the Lord, but was a beautiful Christian woman who made a great impression on my life and lived the verses in Titus 2:3-5--"The aged women likewise, that they be in behavior as becometh holiness, not false accusers, not given to wine, teachers of good things. That they teach the young women to be sober, to love their husbands, to love their children, to be discreet, chaste, keepers at home, good, obedient to their own husbands, that the word of God be not blasphemed."

Through Mrs. Washington, I met the author of this book, Marjie, and her friends. I just shared my life with them as Christ had worked in my life. My dear friends I now ask you to receive Christ into your heart as Lord and Saviour. You can do this by knowing first you are a sinner on your way out of the presence of a Holy God. Jesus said, "I am the way, the truth, and the life; no man cometh unto the Father but by me" (John 14:6). "But as many as received Him, to them gave He the power to become the sons of God, even to them that believe on His name" (John 1:12).

Right now, if you are not a Christian, ask Jesus Christ to come into your heart. Please do not put it off another day. Jesus Christ died on the cross for our sins and paid the price with His life and blood for the debt we owed. When you have received Jesus Christ into your heart, the Bible says: "Therefore, if any man be in Christ, he is a new creature; old things are passed away; all things are become new."

Now you have two natures inside you. The old nature (you) and the new nature (you) and there will be a battle second by second. We call the old nature (flesh) and the new nature (spirit). The flesh would like to rule your life and the Spirit would like to rule. Who will you yield to? It will be one or the other. When the flesh rules, you do not please God. When the Spirit rules, God is pleased.

Let's just say you are a new Christian and you tell a lie. The flesh has ruled and you have sinned, but God knew all about it and gave us a promise to help us walk with Him: 1 John 1:9 "If we confess our sins, He is faithful and just to forgive us our sins, and to cleanse us from all unrighteousness." All we do is agree with God about our sins.

Now that you are a Christian and you mean business when you asked Christ into your heart, it is a once and for all decision. You do not have to keep asking Christ into your heart because you feel you are not a Christian. As Christians we need to grow in the Lord. When you receive Christ, you are a new born child. Children need milk to grow. 1 Peter 2:2, "As newborn babies desire the sincere milk of the word, that ye may grow thereby." There are so many Christians who have remained babies and, worst yet, they don't care!

We need to read the Bible daily. We need to pray, to talk to God daily. We need to witness, to tell others about Jesus, how He died for them and lives in us for God's glory. We need to confess our sins and turn from them. We need to fellowship with other believers in a Bible teaching church regularly, not only when we feel like it. This is how a Christian grows. This is what God is demanding from His children whom He loves and has died and risen again, and is coming back again for!

"Also I heard the voice of the Lord saying, whom shall I send and who will go for us? Then said I, here am I; send me." Isaiah 6:8

To this particular missionary and to others God has planted in various vineyards, I thank God. They were the ones God used to plant the seed in me to commit to full time Christian service. I heard their stories, their testimonies, saw their slides, and viewed their lives committed to our Almighty Saviour. The Lord used people like Beverly to impress upon my life His words, "Yes, I want you to be a missionary too." I didn't know how; I didn't know when; I didn't know where; I was only fourteen at the time. God has His own time table. Little did Beverly know that 20 years later those same seeds planted would find the young woman who was seeing her life, enroute as a missionary to the field of South Africa!

Throughout these twenty years, the Lord continued to remind me of the commitment I made to him to go anywhere. Dave and I married in 1973. Our pastor, Dr. Saxe, would ask Dave and me to accompany him in his ministry to South Africa. "Surely he must be joking," we said. It was in 1988 that God provided the means miraculously for us to accompany Dr. Saxe in the Bible conferences in South Africa. We saw in the eyes of the nationals a different hunger for the things of God. We saw the work of the Lord which was planted by various white missionaries who remain and help establish indigenousness national works. We were asked, aren't there any Black Christians in America who care about our struggles? We replied, "We care." Lord, send us.

Dave battled with surrendering to the call of God. He returned home to the states much like he did when he previously returned from his numerous overseas trips in his years with the Youth For Understanding Choral, touched but not changed. He wanted to make millions for our family. He tried effortlessly at selling water softeners, fire extinguishers, and insurance. David Hill has written a gospel tract entitled, "Hearing the Call of God". Dave knew God was speaking to him. I quietly prayed, and, for those who know me, this was a miracle in itself!

The year David Hill was scheduled to preach at our church, Dave wondered if this could be the same David Hill who wrote the tract. Yes, it was. Dave knew he would soon come face to face with the will of God. While out on visitation, several things were made clear to Dave. That very evening, a brother from southern Africa made a profession of faith in Christ. The reality of the word of God became more evident in our lives. "For it is God which worketh in you to will and to do of His good pleasure" (Philippians 2:13).

God began putting this work of His in our hearts. What about the children people would say? God also began working on their hearts. They had no fears. They knew if God called the parents, He would call and care for them, too. What about all the work that needs to be done for Black people right here in the states others would ask? God is the potter, and we are the clay, vessels for the master's use. If He so wills to use us, where He sees best, what have we to fear or debate? If God be for us, who can be against us?

We attended the TEAM candidate school to prepare for work in the field of South Africa. The work of deputation was difficult. We were reminded, deputation is a ministry. We were also reminded, to talk with God that no breath is lost.... Talk on. To walk with God, no strength is lost....Walk on. To wait for God, no time is lost....Wait on. Echoed over and over were verses such as, "He who began a good work in you will be faithful to complete it" (Phil. 1:6).

God is still calling others into His fields which are already ripe to harvest. Don't be amazed; there will always be scoffers who will think your decision to follow the Lord is utterly insane. Most often the greatest attacks will come from your own family members or others close to you. Satan will use anyone. Yes, it will hurt, resist nursing and rehearsing these hurts. Wait patiently and humbly before God. These situations become stepping stones for higher levels of trust in God, or they become thrown stones by reacting in the flesh. Sowing to the flesh always leads to corruption, but sowing trust and faith in the Spirit leads to life.

It is awesome that the reality of Acts 1:8, "But ye shall receive power, after the Holy Ghost is come upon you: and ye shall be witnesses unto me both in Jerusalem, and in all Judaea, and in Samaria, and unto the uttermost part of the earth" is as much a reality today as it was in the time of the apostles. It is a blessing, as well as, a future reward awaiting those who are sending, going, praying, and giving to the great commission. The Lord Jesus still speaks, "the harvest is plenteous, but the laborers are few" (Matt. 9:37). The cries are still heard, "The harvest is past; the summer is ended; and we are not saved" (Jer. 8:20). "Pray ye therefore the Lord of the harvest, that He will send forth laborers into His harvest" (Matt. 9:38).

DISCUSSION QUESTIONS:

#1   If you were to rate on a scale of 1-10, the quality of mission endeavors, locally, nationally, internationally of your local church, what score would it receive?

#2   What qualities do you think are most important in being a missionary? Is every believer called to be a missionary?

#3   Which fields, (local, nation, foreign) do you feel are most difficult, most challenging, or have the greatest need?

#4   Tell an incident or give a testimony of a missionary you know or have read about.

#5   Today if you or a family member were called of God to a foreign field, how would you respond? What would be the first question you would ask?

Chapter Seven

Chapter Seven
CHANGED INSIDE AND OUT

by Diana Hammuck

"Talk about a child that do love Jesus, here is one." The words of this ole' familiar Negro spiritual reveal what is in my heart. He first loved me. I did not seek Him, for I knew not that I was in need of Him. He had chosen me. Certainly I had heard of Him, was taught of Him and served Him or so I thought, the best I knew how. Somehow, somewhere, along my childhood and teenage life, I was so caught up in being like the crowd to have insight on what it really was to serve the Lord in Spirit and in truth. I did not know I could not live the Christian life without being a true child of God. Whatever I wanted to do, I did. Whatever pleased me and my flesh, I did. I didn't realize as I do now that the flesh cannot be satisfied.

I found myself married at sixteen and divorced before twenty-one with four children who had different fathers. To many this was the norm, yet I knew this was a mess! I was not trained to do anything to make a living for myself, let alone children. I had repeatedly misused my premature adulthood, doing nothing constructive. I did nothing but live day to day not planning or thinking about the future. I worked a few jobs but when ADC (Aid to Dependent Children) failed me or my new male friends were as broke as I, I didn't realize the vicious downward spiral I had got myself caught up in. Sin can take your life and turn it upside down.

I loved my children, and yet at times when I looked at them, I was reminded of my sin. Don't call it sin, and the guilt will go away or you will become desensitized to the whole cycle was the lie Satan tried to sell to me over and over. The occasions I lay with men trying to satisfy longings that could never be satisfied by a moment of sensual pleasure, I used my body seeking to know and experience the difference between love and sex.

LOVE AND SEX ARE NOT THE SAME

LOVE...	SEX...
Is a process.	Is an act.
Requires attention.	Takes little effort.
Is slow growth taking time to develop and evolve.	Is quick, instant a momentary gratification
Is many small behavior changes that bring about good feelings.	Is one big feeling brought by one big behavior.
Involves respect of the person.	Does not require respect of the person.
Has warm laughter & interaction.	The interaction is primarily only physical.
Develops in depth to sustain the relationship.	Yields promises, promises which can't sustain a relation.

I settled for less. What--Who could rescue me from this terrible web I had weaved for myself and only myself I had to blame. "Safe sex" was the answer many said, even way back then. "You're only dumb if you get caught," friends said. Maybe a variety of precautions would have prevented unwanted pregnancies, but no amount of precaution can replace the loss of real intimacy. This life style; it's my choice; it's my bed; I'll just have to lie in it. This is what I told myself to cover the feelings of feeling deserted, cheated, and unfulfilled. It is just doing what comes natural. One almost becomes hypnotized by the body rhythms alluring you to more. From bed to bed, relationship to relationship, if one could really call this having relationships. Why the behavior was no less than glorified relationships like those of the neighborhood pets.

My family filled in as baby-sitters until I misused their kindness and help. I was from a family of eleven children, and I received love and support from my whole family. They would support me in the decision I had to make.

The capital city of Illinois was where we lived. The time was the early 1950s. ADC wasn't so generous to give easily money to support subsequent children, so in order to survive and keep what income I had, I felt I had no choice but to give up two of my babies for adoption. Perhaps I was too immature to think of the total outcome in the long run, but honestly in my heart thought this was the only way to give my children a better chance at life.

With that behind me, now what was to happen with my life? Would I continue this downward trend and see it continue to reproduce itself in future generations of mine? There was a restlessness in me that I could not explain, a want that I could never satisfy. But blessed be the Lord, one day I was invited to attend a revival at a small sanctified church, and, because of nothing better to do that night, I went. Little did I know the Lord God would soon become director of my life. The preacher preached the sermon, entitled "Where Will You Spend Eternity?" The fear of the Lord came over me as the Word of God talked to my soul. My deaf ears were unplugged; my blinded eyes came open; and my mind and heart were broken. Soon the alter call was made. I went forward and cried unto the Lord, "Lord Jesus, forgive me of my many sins!" Praise God, that He did!

Jesus forgave me, washed me, and cleansed me through His blood. He baptized and filled me with His Holy Spirit, and I became a new creature. Old things were passed away, and behold I became new (II Corinthians 5:17). When God through His word spoke directly to my soul, for the first time in my life I was experiencing His love...What amazing love! I knew I had become a new creation. I immediately no longer desired to be with the men nor the crowd I once kept company with. I no longer wanted to visit the places I used to attend. I no longer desired nor had passions which had enslaved me. I no longer wanted to live as I used to live. In fact the "old" me had died. I was crucified with Christ; nevertheless I live, yet not I, but Christ liveth in me; and the life which I now live by the faith of the Son of God who loved me and gave Himself for me (Gal. 2:20).

How can a dead person live? I no longer felt the suffering and guilt. How can a dead person feel pain? However, the pain I caused my family, my own offspring, the pain that the Lord Jesus Himself felt on the cross of Calvary was real pain. I now know the snowball effect of the great sins I committed would affect others for generations to come. The lifestyle we live has an impact on future generations unless these strongholds are not broken. The greatest discovery is the grace of God which is sufficient for all situations.

I began daily to allow the new creation to live in me. "And that He died for all, that they which live should not hence-forth live unto themselves, but unto Him which died for them and rose again" (II Cor. 5:15). I began to desire the things of God; fellowshipping in prayer, praise, and worship to Jesus who had saved me from the penalty of sin, the power of sin, and one day from the very presence of sin. A true child of God will desire the things of God, His wishes, His ways for my life. I had everything to lose (my old lifestyle) and everything to gain. Scoffers said, "She won't last. She'll return to her old life style." Little did they know the secret to success lie in the reality of the scripture Romans 6: 11-14a, "Likewise reckon (to count, to regard) yourselves to be dead indeed unto sin, but alive unto God through Jesus Christ our Lord. Let not sin therefore reign in your mortal body, that ye should obey it in the lusts thereof. Neither yield ye your members as instruments of unrighteousness unto sin: but yield yourselves unto God, as those that are alive from the dead, and your members as instruments of righteousness unto God. For sin shall not have dominion over you."

For over thirty years, I have attended the same church and have been instrumental in many church projects. I have taught Sunday school, been superintendent of summer Bible school, church secretary, choir member, organizer of young women's clubs and a mother of the church both locally and nationally in the church conventions. I have participated in street meetings, visited prisons, have worked in hospitals and nursing homes and private home ministries sharing the love of God. I have spoken at almost every church of many denominations all over my city and surrounding areas. I have been a witness that Jesus truly is the son of God and He does save and keep a person from sin. This is the message I proclaim to African-American women everywhere. There is no reward greater in my life than to teach and share what Christ can do for the many women everywhere who are stuck in fornication and lack of self worth. The God of the Bible through the person of Jesus Christ is still standing at the door of hearts wanting to come in and change your life inside and out!

Not flesh or my flesh, nor bone of my bone but miraculously my own. Never forget for a single minute you didn't grow under my heart, but in it.

Hallelujah is what I add to this testimony, for without it I would not exist as I am today. You see, I am one of the children she gave away for adoption. She had a choice and she chose life not abortion. Adoption allowed me to be placed in a Christian home to another mother who would often voice that God had loaned me to her....a special gift, chosen....I never once had regrets or animosity towards my biological parentage. I rejoice in God's sovereigness to still be able to accomplish His eternal purposes in the lives of those He knew before we were formed (Psalms 71:6).

I agree with the slogan "choose adoption, choose life." There are many struggles adoptees go through. Sometimes, these struggles are expressed. Sometimes, they are suppressed. However these struggles, feelings must be processed. As long as the adopted child is nurtured and loved in a God-honoring atmosphere she will never lose sight of the fact that it is a privileged to have been born of one womb and cared for by another. This links us with one of the greatest examples of adoption. where God our Father adopted us by the work of Jesus Christ into the family of God (Ephesians 1:5).

Many adopted children will not only be inquisitive about their biological heritage but have a certain amount of unrest about who they really are. Knowing and growing up early with a healthy view of adoption will lay a secure foundation for the time when full disclosure is given. A little information given in doses according to the maturational level of the child will help the child accept the findings about his/her biological roots and never lose sight of the love and security based in the parents who raised them. One of the greatest fears for the adopted child is perhaps s/he was given away because there was something wrong with them. Let the child know that it was a loving choice to be given up. Adoption is not a curse.

There may be times when the child will displace anger on the parents who raised them. But rarely ever will the adopted child forget that the adoptive parent(s) chose "me". This special union did not occur by "accident." Adoptive parents can ease the situation by keeping things relaxed and open. Collect biological information for the child's questions that will arise naturally.

As adopted children we hardly gave the issue of adoption much thought. We were loved and cared for. I guess this was what really mattered. Others knew and they would talk! "You had better tell the children," our relatives demanded. After mimicking and mocking our mother for scolding us because we had not tidied our rooms, she returned with tears and compassion in her eyes to tell us, biologically we were not of her and our father, but sovereignly and especially chosen through adoption. I was age eleven; my brother was age thirteen at the time of this disclosure. Gasp!! was our initial response. Then, we all cried and fell into the embracing arms of our mother.

By the time I was eighteen, I was able to notify my biological mother who kept a small box of memorabilia just in case she was ever asked. She presented me with two small photographs of my biological father, whom she had since lost all contact with. I looked long and hard at the photo. How handsome he looked in his sailor uniform. I would often search for this unknown face in crowded bus or airport terminals. She lived in Illinois. I lived in Michigan. He lived in California. The *Springfield Voice*, the hometown newspaper had featured

Dave and my wedding. From here he knew I was living in Ann Arbor.

While lecturing at a series at the University of Berkeley, a young woman from Ann Arbor went forward to ask a question. Trusting her, he explained he had a daughter living in Ann Arbor. Would she mind taking a message to her he asked. My doorbell rang. A salesperson I presumed. No, she had a message from my biological father: "....I don't want to interfere in your life. I don't really have anything to offer. I only want you to know now what I wanted you to know at conception. I am your father. I have always loved you. I always will. I am so very proud of you." He enclosed his phone number in case I ever wanted to make contact.

We made contact by phone and by writing letters and even exchanged photos from the twenty years we had missed. I never had a chance to see him in person. My greatest regret will be if he and my other biological family members enter into an eternity without a personal relationship with the Lord Jesus Christ, I will never be able to unite with them.

When the time for disclosure occurs, all family members need to be considered, adoptive parents, biological parents, and subsequent siblings. Everyone's emotions have to be considered. My biological father located me three years later, when I was twenty-one. Once disclosure occurs the adopted child needs to be spiritually prepared to forgive and love unconditionally. One set of parents might give birth, but the other set births life!

FOR DISCUSSION:

#1 Pregnancy crisis centers are a real help to women in various situations. They are in constant need of Christian women who are armed and prepared to help. Are you aware of a local agency in your area?

#2 Hundreds of children stand in need of adoption or temporary foster care. In what ways can Christian families help?

#3 What might be some of the fears adopted parents or children feel?

#4 In what ways do some of our past life styles catch up with us?

#5 How can believers play a part in helping to restore the ills of problem pasts?

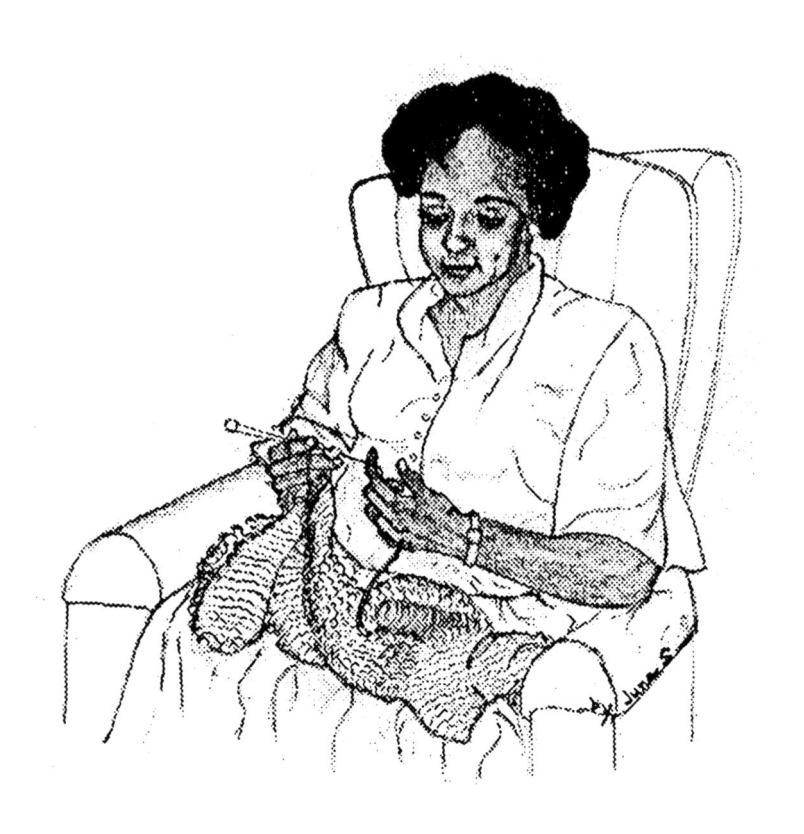

Chapter Eight

Chapter Eight
A LETTER WRITTEN TO GOD

by Ruby Fields

I was asked to give my testimony, but I am a person who doesn't give my testimony too often; I'd rather live it. Yet when I realize what the Lord has done for me, I can't help but share it especially if He can use these words to help someone else.

I was born and reared in a small southern town, Aberdeen, Mississippi. I am the second oldest of six children. As far back as I can remember, I have always been in Sunday school and church. I remember saying when I was young there were two things I wanted; one to get a new bike and the other was to get "religion." In a couple of years, I did. I obtained a bike and my understanding of being a Christian was "getting religion." "Getting religion" meant sitting on the front row of seats of the church which was called the mourners' bench. Everyone would gather around and sing and pray until the mourner got up and shook the minister's hand. There was a song we used to sing, "you've got the Spirit of God; you've got the Spirit of God; if you just open your mouth, if you just cry one time, you've got the Spirit of God...." You guessed it; I opened my mouth; I cried, got up and shook hands with the minister, and left the mourners' bench. I was about nine years-old. For years I just knew I was a Christian because I had "gotten religion."

Some years later after this experience, I got married and left Mississippi and moved to Michigan. I was only sixteen years-old. There was parental objection, especially from my dad. My husband was also a teenager, sixteen years-old. My dad threatened to whip me and told me not to return home. We didn't "have" to get married, but I knew I loved James and wanted to spend the rest of my life with him. Now, I know, there was so much I missed marrying so young, education, life experiences, and so on. It took just about a month and my parents accepted the situation and through the Grace of God, James and I beat the odds of statistics where teenage marriages fail, and we have been married now for over forty years!

After moving to Michigan, my mother told me to get a Bible and join a church. So I did. I went forward one Sunday morning on my Christian experience and was voted in as a member. With my religion I could dance, miss church, go to movies, or anywhere else, smoke, you name it, and it never bothered me. As I look back, I can see why. There really wasn't a change in me. I don't ever remember hearing the gospel. I didn't know what it meant to be saved or to accept Christ as Lord of my life. This really began to bother me. I was a so-called Christian, and there wasn't too much difference in the lives of the other so-called Christians I saw either. So for years I was quite comfortable. Then one summer something happened. There was a split in the church I was attending. I left with the new group to start a new work. We began getting good sound Bible teaching and preaching. Well, I just knew I was saved, so it was only a matter of growing and obeying the Word. But this was not true. It seemed as though God had His time to bring me to a fork in the road. You see it is possible to have your name on the church rolls and working in the church and STILL NOT BE SAVED!

Within a few years the Lord began to deal with me. I began to really hear the gospel. My ears were open. I began to have doubts, wondering if I truly were saved or not. The thought kept haunting me. I didn't say anything or talk to anyone. Why I was a grown woman, I was respected in the church, my children were in high school and college, I had worked and held offices in the church, I had even taught the most vibrant Sunday school classes and DVBS.

I was too ashamed; I had too much pride. That pride almost carried me to Hell. I can understand why the Lord said, suffer the little children to come unto me.... He knows it is easier and they are not taunted or marked by the world. God was so kind and merciful. He was patient; He loved me so much. I finally came to the fork in the road; this point of my life, I had to make a decision. It was up to me. Which way would I choose?

It was during a revival week that God used the pastor's message to make it so plain that even a fool could not err. From this message this is how I saw myself.... There was a large hole in the ground, and it was burning. Stretched across the hole of fire was a piece of cheese cloth. On top of the cloth was myself. The cloth was the only thing between me and Hell. Standing away from the hole was Jesus Christ with His arms stretched open, as if to say the cloth, your pride, your own works, your shame, is nothing to stand on, come to me. Jesus said, I am the way the truth and the life no man cometh to the Father but by me. Hell is prepared for the devil and his followers, we don't have to go to Hell, the choice is up to us as individuals. He is not willing that any should perish...(II Peter 3:9).

I began to get nervous and moved about in my seat (under conviction). When the invitation was given, I still sat there and said nothing. Satan really had a hold on me; pride again. The next few weeks were sheer torture for me. The Word of God was really piercing (Hebrews 4:12). I lost weight. I couldn't eat. I didn't fellowship with anyone. I was just plain miserable. Finally one day at home alone, I went into my bedroom, fell on my knees, and cried unto the Lord, "Lord, I know I am not saved; please forgive me for all my sins and pretending to be a Christian, and come into my heart and save me, and let me live for you!" Oh! What peace and joy followed, the heavy load was lifted. Maybe you've heard the song that goes like this, "I am satisfied." I looked at my hands, and my hands looked new. I looked at my feet and they did, too, ever since that wonderful day. "Thank God I'm satisfied." That's an old song, but I can understand it. You don't really have to have new feet or new hands; it's the new heart Christ places in the reborn individual and we begin looking through new eyes   (II Cor. 5:17).

I was very happy for a while, yet there was still more. If I was going to be obedient to the Word of God that I would need to do. I got to the point where I could not witness anymore because I was not yet fully obedient myself. You see I had not followed the Lord in believers' baptism. And I knew I should. Not that baptism was a part of my being saved but an act of obedience. Satan said, you don't really have to, you were baptized as a child. Yes, I went in the water a dry sinner and came up a wet one. The Word of God began to pierce my soul again, don't you want to identify yourself with me? I was a little reluctant and nervous so I bowed my head and asked the Lord to give me a verse that I could claim and stand on. It was during my morning devotion He gave this verse to me--Isaiah 50:7. I went forward and shared my testimony and was baptized. It has not been all smooth sailing, but it certainly has been a joy. A few years later I had to write a very special letter to the Lord (following the letter is an excerpt written by Roberta Dowdy; it is a profile of Ruby for a class assignment.):

> Dear friend, Lord and Savior Jesus Christ; I am writing to you because only you and I really know what I am going through at this time. Friend you have really been a comfort to me during this past month. My Lord, you are the only one who knows me in and out, through and through. You know when I hurt and when I feel good. But nevertheless, you have given me a peace and love for you that I can never explain. During this time you have brought me closer to my family. You have made me more understanding towards others and you have given me a greater desire to share your word. Whatever happens to me you will get the glory out of my life.
>
> Remember when I almost had the doctor to do another scan before I went into the hospital? But you said no, just wait until you go in, so others may know of my great work. You can be a great witness for me there. I almost shared this with all my family. Do you think I should have? Remember how you had to keep comforting and reassuring me in your word with such verses as I Cor. 10:13? You also told me about Job and how I should really trust you completely. I should not doubt or worry. Just give all my anxiety to you. You reassured me again with these words, if I gave you my son, how much more with Him will I freely give you all things. Oh, thank you Lord. Lord, you are such a loving Saviour. You know just whose heart to

burden to pray for me. You knew just what my needs were at a particular time and you met my needs just as you promised.

Thanks for all the words of encouragement that you sent through other vessels, the books, and the thoughts and prayers from daily devotionals. You know as my friend I can never thank you enough. As my Lord I am forever at your beck and call. I willingly volunteer to be your slave. I never would have thought or dreamed that by you carrying me through the valleys of sorrow and pain that I would come out seeing you through new eyes and loving you so much more.

Thank you for carrying me. I could reach out anytime and you were there. You know when I merely had "religion" this relationship was never possible. Thank you for helping me put my priority in order. You told me to seek ye first the kingdom of God and His righteousness and all other things will be added unto me. Now Lord, there is just one other area in my life that I need help with, praying without ceasing. Lord help me to realize that your miracle may be to heal me, but whatever you choose I thank you in advance. Because whatever you do for me I know it will be best for me.

I love you Lord and Friend.

Your servant forever,

Ruby Mae

A PROFILE OF RUBY

"Lord, work a miracle in my life"

This was Ruby's quiet, yet emphatic answer to my question concerning her recent recovery from brain surgery. As she shared her experiences, I watched with thankful awe. Her face was radiant, her eyes sparkled and occasionally glistened as tears of joy spilled from her eyelids. I've known Ruby as a friend for many years. Her Christian testimony has always been a joy to behold for she truly delights herself in the Lord. This most recent experience has caused her to become a richer stalwart of this most precious faith, the faith as found rooted and grounded in the Lord Jesus Christ.

It began seventeen months ago with sharp pains in her head and a numbing sensation on her left side. Her family often teased her about going to the doctor for the least complaint, so they took little notice when she announced an appointment for mid-November. They even forgot to ask the results of that visit which allowed Ruby to keep the diagnosis secret from all but her husband. She told him, but only after she had wrestled with it herself and felt sufficiently capable to share it without causing alarm.

Surgery was the prescribed treatment. A neurosurgeon was to be consulted and further testing would be required. The family doctor had been quite blunt as he told her of her dilemma. "You have a tumor, not too large, but all indications are that it is cancerous!" His voice was abrupt and unfeeling, leaving Ruby emotionally drained. The appointment with the specialist was made and several tests, including a brain scan, were taken. While Ruby waited for results, she busied herself caring for others. A surprise birthday party for her husband was among her activities. As the year 1979 ended, Ruby and James received the opinion of the neurosurgeon, the results of the brain scan and the date for surgery. They had set together to hear the doctor explain the full extent of the surgery and give the results. The interval between their visit to the specialist and the actual surgery, Ruby spent in an attitude of prayer. She petitioned the Lord for His sustaining grace, His perfect will to be done, trusting Him to save her, to heal her body and for the tumor to be non-malignant. It was during this waiting period that Ruby left the crowded background of "say-so" Christians and entered the arena of "do-do" Christians. Her life had been given to Christ earlier, but, during that period of waiting, she yielded her life completely, realizing the truth of Lamentations 3:22-25. "It is of the Lord's mercies that we are not consumed, because His compassions fail not. They are new every morning: Great is Thy faithfulness. The Lord is my portion, saith my soul; therefore will I hope in Him. The Lord is good unto them that wait for Him, to the soul that seeketh Him."

To express her deeper commitment, she wrote a letter to the Lord and sealed it, never dreaming that it would be a source of encouraging comfort and continual revival during the months that followed her surgery. The surgery to remove the growth in her brain required three operations because the negative possibilities occurred. One of her neurosurgeons expressed it this way, "You've been to Hell and back, Ruby." Her trust in the faithfulness of God and reliance upon the promise in His word saw her through the valleys of depressions, periods of physical and mental weakness, and was her strength during the agonizing months of recovery.

To see her now, you'd never know of her traumatic experience except for a small scar at the hairline of her left forehead. A deeper, spiritual maturity is now evident in her life, and she gives God the praise for the miracles He worked in her life. Ruby cherished her family's loving support and the many expressions of love from her church family. She had used the God given opportunities to share her experience with others going through identical or similar surgeries. Her heart is also burdened for those who yet do not know or enjoy the true peace that comes only from God through the Lord Jesus Christ. In her own words, "This experience has made me bolder, stronger in my faith. I'm now always seeking a way to share Christ with someone, beginning with my family and relatives. It has also taught me to cry. I'm more tender, not hardened as before, more sensitive and compassionate to others." Ruby's favorite Bible verse during this experience was Isaiah 50:7 "For the Lord God will help me; therefore shall I not be confounded; therefore, I have set my face like a flint, and I know I shall not be ashamed."

Ruby was my Sunday school teacher. She was faithful to her post. We never in our wildest dreams could have thought she was not a true child of God. But the Lord knows them that are His (II Tim. 2:19). There will be so many on that day who will say, "Lord, didn't we do this in Your name, and didn't we do that in your name? Surely I am good enough for the kingdom. I wasn't that bad.... I was a pretty good member of a local church.... their list will go on, but He will say, ' Depart from me; I never knew you' ."

There are many who fake at being a good Christian, but that won't be good enough for a holy righteous God who has made the way so clear in His word. For any who are heavy hearted because of trials, be they physical or spiritual, may Ruby's testimony be of comfort and may it also challenge you to really come to know that you know the Lord as Savior and trust Him fully in every area of your life.

FOR DISCUSSION:

#1 Nothing is more important than the certainty that "I am saved"--that is, that I have received eternal life by inviting Christ into my life. When people are asked: "Do you know that your sins are forgiven and that you are going to Heaven?" They respond with a number of different answers:

1. I don't know. I don't think anybody knows for sure.
2. I hope so. I try to do my best to please God.
3. I've got my church!
4. I am as good as the next Christian.
5. I think so. I was baptized and my parents are religious.

Which of these answers are sufficient? How would you answer the above question about assurance of salvation?

#2 Study the following scripture references related to salvation assurance:

> I John 5:10-13
> Isaiah 59:1-2
> Romans 3:10,23, 5:8, 6:23, 10:9-10
> Revelation 20:15
> Ephesians 2:8-10

#3 Many people wonder and debate if miracles, wonders, and healings still take place in Christendom. What is your response?

#4 If you were told you only had 1 month to live how would you like to spend those 30 days?

#5 Have you considered preparations for your impending death such as funeral arrangements, wills, and, most importantly, where you will spend eternity?

Reflections of Christian Women

Chapter Nine

Chapter Nine
UNEQUALLY YOKED

by Gloria Brown

I was born the oldest of four children in Jackson, Mississippi. My mother is a Christian and a minister's daughter. My father was a service man who wanted to hit the big cities. So we moved to Chicago. My story is almost like mother like daughter. My mother took us to church and set a good Christian example before us. My father objected, but mother took us anyway. My mother was determined to keep the family together, but, when I was a young teen, my father left and never returned.

I accepted Christ as my personal Savior at the age of nine at an evening church service and it was a real commitment. In the 7th and 8th grades, I became interested in the opposite sex. My mother was very strict, too strict I felt. I used my music, the church choir as a place to get away. Mother tried working, but, because my father had left us, she did the providing which left us more on our own. Yet one thing I can remember is that she held family devotions everyday. Either she or she appointed one of us to read from the Bible and followed with prayer. I'm certain that this is one of the things that kept me close to the Lord.

When it was time for high school, I was determined to really live for the Lord. Pressures to be one of the crowd allowed my Christian testimony to slide downward, but, praise the Lord, never towards drugs, smoking, sex, or drinking. Then it was time for college. I was offered several scholarships in music. My mother did not want me to go far away from home but a full scholarship from Kentucky State was offered and I wanted to get away from the big city, Chicago. Once again I purposed in my heart to serve the Lord and live for Him. I arrived at college and things were going great. I even had a Christian roommate. It was a good first year. Then, I got involved in sororities and at this time sororities on our campus were not some things Christians should have gotten involved in. I was elected music queen and my social life!!!!! I met a Catholic guy, and even my mother said this was not the guy for me. Who wants to listen to her mother? I was enjoying all this new attention. I arrived back at school the new semester, and this other guy had been watching me all the time. He was captain of the football team, a real popular guy on campus, and good looking too. He knew the Catholic fellow was on my trail, but, since the football players and choir members arrived on campus earlier than the other students, we developed a relationship. Mr. Pro football would show up at my recital and said he always wanted a wife who could sing and play the piano. I told him I did not want a husband who smoked or drank or ran around. His senior year found him with a broken leg and out from football for the season. He proposed the question of marriage. I told him I wanted to marry a Christian. He said he could tell I was different. I told him it was because I was a Christian and Christians should be different. He told me he had accepted Christ as a teenager. Great, I said. So now things really looked rosy. Momma said, "Be sure this is the person the Lord wants you to have."

We had to have a small wedding. Momma didn't have a lot of money. But that didn't bother me. I was so ecstatic; then, one day I remember calling momma crying because we had a big argument. I called off the wedding about one month before the due date. Momma had pinched and saved buying things in preparation for the wedding. She said, however, that it was not a waste of money if this marriage was not God's will. Well, we patched things up, and the wedding was on again.

The following year I finished school. We lived and worked on a boys camp in Ohio. The boys were ages 9-18 and had committed crimes from petty theft to murder. He was teaching physical education, and I was teaching English. It was nice working together. We knew some of the guys there committed crimes just to get sentenced to this camp, where at least three meals were served and there was a place to rest. I also had a chance to work with the chaplain. We had a boys choir. It was a rewarding experience to see some of the boys come to know the Lord. Others went away bitter.

Later my husband and I became involved in a pyramid sales program. Our entire savings went into this investment, and, of course, we were on our way to making it rich. We left Ohio and returned to Chicago. I guess trouble followed. I was expecting our first baby. We stayed with my aunt. My husband felt like a failure. Relatives and their comments did not help. All those unsalable products and progressing nowhere. So he sought employment through the Chicago school board. Now we were on our way back. A two bedroom apartment was the next step and by then we had two sons and boom! the doctor said we were having twins! Yet praise the Lord I hardly ever had to work outside the home. I could be with the children and soon the twins would be in school and our husband/father had been our provider.

In Ohio we were going to church together and even praying together. There the church had a basketball team and golf associates but in Chicago my home church really turned him off. Oh how church members have to be careful how we entertain strangers who come among us for worship. Then, to my amazement my husband told me he really was not a Christian and that his friends made him go forward in a church service. He said he believed in God and he was a good man. I believed in God and also believed my husband was a very good man, but that wouldn't save him.

Then, there was the day a man gave my husband a leaflet, and he began attending some of their meetings. Certainly he was searching. God knows and so does the devil. This was a cult group. This went on for several years. The children attended services with me, and I thanked the Lord each day that he had no objections. Our two sons accepted the Lord as their personal savior and they wondered why daddy wasn't with us and hadn't accepted the Lord as we. I never wanted them to look down on their father but I would tell them just continue to pray for him.

One day the children and I were out on a picnic. When we returned home, we saw neighbors gathered around our house which was smoked-filled. A neighbor said my husband had been burned and taken to the hospital with the nearest burn unit. One neighbor watched the children, and another took me to the hospital. The doctor met me and gave me the condition of my husband. There was constant changing of bandages for he was burned from his top trunk to his legs. He was hospitalized for two months. Now, my faith was to be tried. The doctors said he could die, not from the burns but from the complications. There were serious problems that did arise during recuperations. I can praise the Lord for the prayers that went up on his behalf. I can remember my mother's words (II Peter 3:9): "God is not willing that any should perish but that all should come to repentance." She gave me faith that my husband would not be taken until he could acknowledge Jesus as Lord and his personal Savior. The Lord healed his body, and we are still praying for us to totally be one in the Lord as we are one in the flesh.

I am the music director of my church but going every night or too much church activity is out. I have to limit myself so that I can be with him who I love and my duties at home. James 1:2-4 said, "my (sisters) count it all joy when ye fall into various trials, knowing this, that the testing of your faith worketh patience. But let patience have her perfect work, that ye may be perfect and entire lacking nothing."

To me and other Christian women who are unequally yoked, we need to be joyful. We can be happy and joyful in spite of the situation. My marriage won't end, and, sure, I have sinned but Christ forgives. That is something I really had to get over, blaming my husband when it was my fault. I was out of the Lord's will. Psalm 51 says, "Create in me a clean heart and renew in me a right spirit." Trust God to make that wrong situation work for His glory. And heed to what James says, to be patient. I especially have to remember this when I get anxious being the spiritual head in the home. I long as so many women do to see their husbands leading in spiritual matters in the home and in the church. Oh God, help our men!!! I say to myself, Lord why don't you save him right now? I realize even Christian marriages have some of the same problems as marriages that are unequally yoked, but we as the Christian mates have to be constantly changing. Matthew 5:16 says, "Let your light so shine before men (our mates) that they may see your good works and glorify your father who is in heaven."

"Likewise ye wives, be in subjection to your own husbands: that if any obey not the word, they also may without the word be one by the conversation of the wise; while they behold your chaste conversation coupled with fear, whose adorning let it not be that outward adorning of plaiting the hair, and wearing of gold, or of putting on of apparel; but let it be the hidden man of the heart, in that which is not corruptible, even the ornament of a meek and quite spirit, which is in the sight of God a great price." 1 Peter 3:1-4

Surveys show few Black men attend church. One out of three women attend church at least once a week. Only one out of five Black men attend church. Reasons stated for non attendance are: men are made to feel inferior to the minister who is often placed on a pedestal. Others said going to church was considered irrelevant and unmanly.

A 1990 Gallop Poll reported, Blacks as a whole still continue to place religion high on the list of priorities. In fact, 75% of Blacks supported the idea that religion is the solution to problems today. Even a 1992 issue of *Ebony* reported, the most eligible bachelorettes still preferred 3 to 1 a God-fearing Black male companion.

How does a Christian woman respond to a non-Christian husband? Often, there is much frustration heard from Christian African-American women who long for a Spirit-filled African-American man to take positions of order under the leadership of an almighty shepherd, Jesus Christ, Himself, and be loved as Christ loved the church. Only in submitting ourselves one to another as unto the Lord can we accomplish God's original purpose.

The man is capable and can be empowered to be able to lead his family in daily devotions, to be the first to suggest that the family has prayer, to lead his family to the house of God for worship. All of this is possible if we as women would follow the principles of God in 1 Peter. Satan knows that a family the principles of God in 1 Peter. Satan knows that a family committed to God and each other is a dynamic force that cannot be reckoned with. It is a high calling, a mark we can press towards together. Take back the family and the order God originated to be a victorious family for Christ. "We are more than conquerors through Jesus Christ our Lord."

DISCUSSION QUESTIONS:

#1 What are some of the greatest struggles faced being married to a non-Christian mate?

#2 In what ways can the church assist women who are in marriages which are unequally yoked?

#3 Discuss the following scripture passages; II Cor. 6:14 and I Cor. 7: 10-16.

Chapter Ten

Chapter Ten
IN HIS TIME

by Jacquelin Wright

My name is Jacqueline Wright. I am the second to the oldest of four siblings. At a very early age I was taught from my parents that my relationship to the Lord and prayer was the key to happiness. "But without faith it is impossible to please Him. For he that cometh to God must believe that he is and that He is a rewarder of them that diligently seek Him" (Hebrews 11:6).

It is important for mothers and fathers to instruct their children in the things of God early. Daughters can be taught as early as in their primary years to begin praying for that little boy who will some day, God willing, be their mate. Pray that he is being nurtured and brought up in the Lord by Godly parents. My parents sought to teach us early to entrust our future to the guidance of an almighty God who faileth not.

I've been waiting a long time by the world's standards to get married. I dated occasionally, I've gone on a few blind dates, and even once joined a dating service, never meeting Mr. Right. I guess the biggest hardship in being single all of these years was all the negativeness from the world and yes, even from Christians. "What's wrong with Jackie...she's pretty, intelligent. What's her problem?" "You're too picky, just go ahead and marry." And I am certain there were things being said behind my back, and you can just imagine what was said, that I don't even care to mention. I had to develop a sense of humor to deal with some of this negativeness. At a gathering I was asked, "Where is your husband?" "Why you'll have to ask God that question," I responded with a smile. Oh yes, there were times when I hurt. Christians need to be more sensitive to one another's needs. By the time I was twenty, all of my associates were married. It was difficult to read the newspaper and see all the ages and names of people getting married. Being at family gatherings were difficult periods. Family members can be so insensitive. Some churches lack programs and members lack communication skills to effectively meet the needs of singles.

As a Christian woman holding to Godly principles, I didn't really fit in with the conversations of other women who had gone through passages of childbirth, school, teen years, etc. Topics discussed by other women included their flings with males at bars, in bedrooms, the latest soaps, or trashy magazines.

I thank God for other blessings I received: health, clear skin and body tone, mental and spiritual fulfillment, all things I could enjoy with or without having a serious relationship. The most important thing I had to remember was to live my life God's way. God asked me through His word to keep my bed undefiled, to live holy, and to delight myself in Him and He would give me the desires of my heart (Ps. 37:4). "Marriage is honorable and the bed is undefiled but whoremongers and adulterers God will judge" (Hebrews 13:4). I've done what God asked me to do. I practiced praying before going on dates. "Make no provision for the flesh." Even in my older age, I always had my dates escort me home to my parents' home - not to my own home. I did not watch movies, television programs, or listen to music that permeated the lust of the flesh. Sex is not just intercourse. Touching like you are a married couple is also a danger to avoid. Any level of intimacy is temptation. Too many underestimate the power of the flesh.

During my high school years, I didn't think too much about marriage. I wanted to get more education and perhaps date for a while and take time to focus on who I was. I'd heard it said, "Marriage is not two halves seeking to become whole, but two whole persons who are willing to blend their wholeness into a new unity." Marriage is more than finding the right partner....it's being the right partner!

After graduation, I attended Glen Oaks Community College, earning an Associates in Business. I held several good jobs, one at Michigan Power, another at Essex Wire as a claims coordinator. I began to focus on my strengths and to express all of my doubts and fears about my future. Where should I live? What car should I drive? What about other financial decisions? I trusted God's word--Philippians 4:19: "But my God shall supply all your need according to His riches in glory by Christ Jesus."

My biggest encouragement through all these years has been from my family, my dad, my sisters, my brother, and, especially, my mom. They have prayed for and with me and kept the faith that God would deliver in His time. Well, I am forty-one years-old, and my bed has never been defiled. In other words, I am a virgin and very proud that God has kept me! This year I am getting married!!!

Going into 1992, I changed my prayer. Before I told God what I wanted...tall, dark, handsome, etc. Now, instead of telling Him, I asked Him to tell me what He wanted for my life...married to Mr. Right, or single and content! Through years of dating, I was just not meeting Mr. Right. But once I turned it completely over to Him, I received my gift.

One day a girlfriend called and asked me if I would like to meet someone she knew from work. I was familiar with this scenario. I said, "ok." She told me to call her later on in the week to confirm the day and time. I took a personal day off from work and drove to her place of work, had a tour and waited for lunch. What went through my head was praise. Yes, I had prayed before I left home for traveling mercies. It was a crisp, yet beautiful February day. I also asked God to make the directions easy to follow because I am absolutely terrible when it comes to traveling to strange places. The Lord got me there safely and on time with a few minutes to spare. Oh, yes, I reviewed my prayer, "Lord, I've always liked tall good looking men, who dressed sharp, had a fine education, a nice car and saved!!"

Well, you see how worldly my mind was, I mentioned saved at the end. I repented to the Lord, "Lord, you know me better than I know myself." The important thing is that He loves you, and, if he loves you, I know he will love me. Where was my mind! My girlfriend hadn't even sat down to lunch yet, and I was way ahead of the ball game. Just at that point she said, "There he goes now!" She walked over to him and then brought him over to our table. As they were walking towards the table, I drifted, thinking to myself, he's too short; he's not my type. In no time, he was standing in front of me being introduced.

I looked at him. He had the sweetest smile, a radiance. These were not qualities I usually saw first. I thought wow! This guy is really sweet and nice. I proceeded to move my coat so he could have a seat, but he said he would not be staying. He picked up a few items to eat at his desk. That was the end of that, or so I thought.

Well, on my way back home, I thought at least I got a chance to get out of my small town for a few hours, and I needed a break from work. I thanked God for such a lovely day and for taking me back and forth safely. I took time to think about my involvement in the lives of my family members and in the life of my church family. I led in children's church as well as in the ministry of foster child care in my parents' home. I also taught in women Bible classes. So many women in the church were not grounded in the basic Bible truths. They attended church regularly, perhaps quoted Psalm 23 and John 3:16 and sang "Standing on the Promises," without knowing what they were. I was so burdened for these women. Satan tried to tell me as he oft times did before, you missed everything now. You had your opportunity to be married. Was being married a greater work or was the ministry that I was involved in as a single the greater work? Who was measuring? God's will, God's standards were always best.

Later on that evening, I received a call from my friend who attempted the introductions at lunch time. She said that Ken wanted my telephone number. I didn't believe her. Are you sure? At first I thought, no. Then I said sure. He called; we talked; he wanted to take me to dinner and apologized for not staying for lunch. He didn't know I came to be introduced. After about three telephone calls, we met for dinner. I had a lot of reservations. I was going to hurry up, eat, and get out of there. That didn't happen. I was totally impressed. He stood up as he spotted me. With that nice smile he made me feel special. He opened the door for me, adjusted my seat, and was a real gentleman.

After dinner we went to my parents' house. I introduced him. After that date, he called regularly, and we both established what we wanted....just friendship. In hind sight, I see the truth of the quote on many a wedding invitation, today is the day I marry "my friend." Our friendship grew. One of the reasons I believe it grew was because from the first time we went out and afterwards, we prayed over our meals together and over our friendship. Kenneth and I met in February. He asked me to marry him on May 30th. We will be married on September 5, 1992.

No, Kenneth is not real tall. He is smart, one of the smartest men I know, but he doesn't have a degree. God's wisdom is not measured by acquiring a Ph.D. or Th.D. He doesn't spend money on fancy cars or clothes for himself. He spends money on others who are in need. I began to see the qualities of a saved man, a reality of his relationship to the Lord Jesus Christ, gentleness, meekness, joy, and selflessness were real desired qualities. I thanked God He picked my husband for me because I couldn't have picked a better man.

I've always believed that God has the best gift for each one of us from the time we are born. However for some people, it takes longer to receive their gift. It's like at Christmas time. Have you ever seen a Christmas tree full underneath with presents? All kinds of wrapping, sizes, and colors. You go to pick one. You are impressed with the outer wrapping, the beautiful bows, and even the size. Certainly the most ostentatious, the greater the gift. Life can be that way sometimes. Here we have a choice of presents under the tree. We have our wants, our ideas of what is best. By happenstance, we reach over to an unassuming package, perhaps not as desirable as the rest, lost in our own desires, we almost miss what is best...God's choice. You open this gift and all kinds of beautiful qualities are inside. Yes, I am reminded of Christ where it was said of Him, "He was comely that no one should desire Him." Much of the world has yet to see Him, God's gift to us because He's not wrapped/packaged according to their standards. At judgment, they will be left missing the best gift. "Thanks be unto God for His unspeakable gift" salvation through the Lord Jesus Christ. Often I have heard many African-American men complain that all a sister wants is to know what size bank account the brother has. Is he dressed so fine? What kind of car does he drive? The demands go on. Many a brother is left wondering whether he is valued for who he is or only for what he has. Too many sisters are foremost worried about getting that they forget relationships are also about giving. The plight of the Black man doesn't have to be repeated or exploited in the media for Black women to get to the point where we admit, we need to love our Black men. God reminds us from His word, "All good and perfect gifts come from above"....In His time....and I plan on loving mine!

I ask the Lord the same questions I am asked about my future husband. He is divorced with two teenage sons. I struggled with the questions of God's will regarding marriage, divorce, and remarriage. I sought the Lord fervently. I felt Him responding, "You asked me to pick out the right man. You've asked for the gift of marriage. Now, that I have given you my choice, you're still asking me questions."

Ken received Christ as his personal saviour after his divorce. He remained celibate, which is rare in the times in which we live in today. God brought other mature Christians who counseled and confirmed my decision about this relationship. I rested my questions and bathed my doubts in verses found in I Cor. 7: 10-17, 24-26, "Art thou bound to a wife? Seek not to be loosed. Art thou loose from a wife? Seek not a wife. But and if thou marry, thou hast not sinned; and if a virgin marry she hath not sinned" (I Corinthians 7:27-28).

I realize at this age I have become a very independent woman. At the same time, my father has always been the spiritual head in my home. Now, I will have to submit to a new spiritual headship. My needs will not necessarily come first. Relationships with my nephews has equipped me to handle the ministry of step-parenting. Being around family and my church family has helped me to share and give.

A long time ago, I asked the Lord to be the master conductor of my life. I played a solo for a long time. He has now asked me to play a duet with Ken, one song ...for His glory and ...in His time.

"Fear thou not: For I am with thee. Be not dismayed; for I am thy God. I will strengthen thee: Yea I will help thee; Yea I will uphold thee with the right hand of my righteousness." Isaiah 41:10

One out of every three adults in America is single. The high statistics regarding divorce bear no secrets. Single female headed households among African-American women in most circles has become the norm. Widowhood and remaining single by choice encompass the figures of those in the Christian community, who may be single but not alone. Christ has promised, "I will never leave thee, nor forsake thee" (Hebrews 13:15). God's word further instructs us that singleness can be profitable (I Corinthian 7:32-35).

Our value and self-worth are not determined by the acceptance or rejection of our fellowmen. Not even by the tremendous hurt of being rejected by a mate. Our worth is rooted in the declaration that we are the children of God.

As singles, avoid falling into the habit of singing the single blues. This brings about pessimism which cramps creativity. That is not to say the pessimism is not justified. Many times it is. Our human nature since creation was designed for fellowship, for close communication with God and our fellow man. Loneliness is a real feeling. And yet we all have to learn to distinguish the difference between physical loneliness and psychological loneliness. Many a married person suffers psychological loneliness. I am so grateful to singles who have touched my life: Rebecca Ann Dandridge, Sandra Weeden, Iverna Shelton, Betty Allen, Betty Duffin, Lisa Smith, Lynette White, and others, who in their own circumstances of singleness have been ones who have made a difference for the kingdom of God. They have shown me truly we need each other.

Don't allow loneliness to manifest itself in depression, grief, feelings of rejection, or into bouncing relationships. For certainly, there is something worse than not being married, and that is being married to the wrong person. Do an attitude check. Is your singleness making you bitter or better? Make yourself available. Is your singleness an asset or ashpot with no glow, available. Is your singleness an asset or ashpot with no glow, avoiding church fellowship, resenting others because of their coupleness? This is the problem that a negative attitude about singleness does, it produces lethargy. Pessimism, also, perpetuates our past. A pessimist is one who looks at failures and expects only more. It is a painful prison from which one cannot break free. In addition, pessimism casts a dark shadow of impossibility over our future. Instead, a positive spirit thanks God for the past, good or bad, realizing even failures can become building blocks. After thanking God, trust God with what He can do in your future.

There are numerous examples in the Bible of singles who took their singleness as greater opportunity for service. More than ever before, singles, whether by choice or circumstance, have an awesome opportunity to be effective Christians in the church. The total body of Christ has to add to our awareness of the single adult population, their unique problems, untapped potential which is vital to the total church ministry.

DISCUSSION QUESTIONS:

#1   Do you feel the needs of singles are being met in your church?

#2   In what ways can singles avoid feeling like or being a burden?

#3   In what ways is singleness a blessing?

#4   If God is the master "match- maker" then a single person desiring a mate doesn't have to seek a mate, but seek God who knows the mate He has for you. How is this accomplished?

#5   What are some practical ways of dealing with feelings of loneliness?

Reflections of Christian Women

Chapter Eleven

Chapter Eleven
DREAMS DO COME TRUE

by Arlene Thomas

As a confused twelve year-old I was looking for peace and happiness. It was difficult living in a home with an alcoholic father who was at times abusive to my mother physically and mentally. Things in my home could and did change in a moments notice due to my father's drinking and mood changes. When my father wasn't drinking he was kind and sweet, but his drinking problem made him a totally different person.

Although my mother did not have a personal relationship with Jesus Christ, she wanted to raise her children with Christian principles. She insisted on my going to Sunday school. I really enjoyed the times at church. I sang in the youth choir and enjoyed hearing the preacher and Sunday school teacher talk about Heaven. At the young age of twelve, I realized that I was not a true Christian. The people at the church I attended lived ungodly during the week and pretended to be holy on Sunday. I didn't want to be a hypocrite. True salvation was not preached at the church I was a member of.

I got baptized because I was told I might get into heaven if I did. I wanted to be saved, but I also realized that serving God would not be easy. It would take sacrifice. I felt it would be too difficult to live for Christ on my own and at such a young age, so I asked the Lord to give me a godly husband when I grew up. It's funny because I asked for specific characteristics in this husband, someone who didn't smoke or drink, who would treat me nice and be a true Christian. Oh yes, I asked God that he would be good looking too! I promised God that if he gave me this husband, I'd live for Him. How soon I forgot my promise to God. As a teenager I got involved with a boy who was in the likeness of my father. We dated seriously through my high school years. Could this possibly be the husband I had prayed for? Would God save him?

My mother and father provided for all of our material needs. As a family of seven we lived in a small two bedroom home in Roseville, Michigan near Detroit. My father worked hard as a factory worker. My mother worked as a maid in my younger years, but then got a job at a major hospital in the housekeeping department. I wanted more for myself. I dreamed of the typical American middle class dream: a nice home, two cars, and two kids. College was the answer. Western Michigan University was my school of choice. In my second week of college, I met this very nice guy named Michael. Before long we became good friends. He was different from any other guy I had met. In time I found out that he was a Christian. He told me the plan of salvation and that the only way we could continue to date was if I accepted Christ as my personal saviour. For a while I pretended to be a Christian, but Michael knew that I hadn't accepted Christ in my heart. "Therefore if any man be in Christ he is a new creature" (II Cor, 5:17). He stopped dating me because I was not saved. "Do not be bound together with unbelievers, for what partnership have righteousness and lawlessness or what fellowship has light with darkness" (II Cor. 6:14)? It was really hard for me at first because I wanted to be with Michael. Why couldn't he accept me the way I was? I wouldn't interfere with his relationship with God. Couldn't I serve God in my own way? God in His mercy showed me that I had a greater need than a boyfriend. I needed Christ in my life. The verse that really convinced me was Romans 3:23: "For all have sinned and come short of the glory of God." My Sunday school attendance and baptism at age twelve was not going to save me. I had to accept Christ into my heart. I bowed my head and prayed, "Lord I know I am a sinner, my sin separates me from God. Jesus Christ paid the price for my sin on the cross of Calvary to insure my salvation. I accept by faith the finished work of Jesus Christ." I received Him as my personal saviour. Now I was a real Christian! A month later, Michael started dating me again, and, after three years of dating, we were married November 17, 1979.

How happy I was to be married. God had answered the prayer I said as a twelve year-old girl. Michael was everything I had asked God for and more. Now, it was up to me to fulfill my promise to God. It was time for me to live for Him. Michael told me that he felt the Lord had called him into the ministry.

I was very afraid of this as I associated being in the ministry with being poor. It seemed to me that all the truly dedicated men of God did without material things. I had seen how missionaries and ministers were given second-hand clothes and lived in houses they never owned. This was not the American middle class dream that I wanted so badly. How could Michael do this to me? Our life was fine the way it was. Wasn't it? In my heart I knew I could not hold Michael back. After all, I had to admit that I was starting to live a mediocre Christian life. I was not living in sin, but I was satisfied with having a nice Christian home and being free from any commitments to truly serve Christ. I needed to be a true disciple of Christ. "Whoever does not carry his own cross and come after me cannot be my disciple" (Luke 14:27). In prayer I surrendered my will and told the Lord to use me in any way He pleased. In making this prayer to God I had much fear in what the future held. I realized that I might be required to give up my dreams, and let God give me the type of life that was best for me.

In January 1982, the Lord blessed us with a beautiful daughter named Andrea. By the time she was two years old, we found out that she had serious eye problems. Her glasses and visits to doctors and specialists were very expensive and more than our budget could afford. It seemed that there were always problems to deal with. The car was always breaking down. We didn't have enough money to pay our bills. When Andrea turned three years old, I lost a child through miscarriage. Not knowing whether the baby was a boy or girl, we gave the baby the name, Tracey Lee. Michael stayed sick with colds, viruses and sickness that even the doctors could not diagnose. Through all of this, Michael and I grew stronger in the Lord. We learned to pray together about our trials. As a young couple, we held on to James 1:2,3: "consider it all joy my brethren, when you encounter various trials, knowing that the testing of your faith produces endurance." In February 1986, Michael told me that we were moving back to his hometown, Detroit. What would become of me there?

When we first moved to Detroit, we stayed with Michael's grandmother. This in itself was a difficult trial. We stayed in the city proper for a full year. We tried to purchase our first home in Rosedale Park, a beautiful section of Detroit, but, two weeks before closing, the deal fell through. We needed a place of our own and so Michael found a nice luxury apartment for a reasonable price in Westland, Michigan.

Life was wonderful now. My dream of being home with our daughter and living in a nice place had come true. I even had a new car to drive. Michael was working with Detroit Public Schools as a teacher and serving the Lord as assistant pastor for a small Baptist church. I was serving in that same church as Sunday school teacher.

In the summer of 1987, the Lord laid on my heart, "be strong and be of good courage"...from Joshua, Chapter 1. I didn't understand exactly what that meant but later it was revealed to me. Michael had decided to go with Baptist Missions of North America, and he would not be returning to his job that September. The Lord brought to my mind how I had surrendered my will to His and that I must pick up my cross and follow Him. This was my chance to show God that I really did believe all those things that I learned in His word through the years. It was time for me to let God's word live through me. I told Michael I would trust God with him to serve the Lord with Baptist Missions of North America. Upon graduation from candidate school, we were told that there were no pastorates available. (Even before candidate school we were told several pastors were waiting to leave their missions' churches to go on to start more churches and they needed men like Michael to step in taking over the pastorate.) We had to come back to Westland with no ministry and no jobs. Day by day times were difficult. We could not pay our rent. Our phone was shut off. Our heat was shut off. We had no car or health insurance. Andrea's eyes took a turn for the worse, and we were told she needed surgery. We had no money to pay for the surgery or the doctor visits. All the things I had taken for granted were now missing. We had to literally wait upon God for our daily bread. I remember many times having only $5.00 to buy groceries for four days. How could this be happening to me? What about my dreams?

It was during this most stressful and difficult time that I learned to pray and to trust God to provide all that I needed. God would always come through with enough blessing to get me through another day. God healed Andrea's eyes after two weeks of prayer by us and our church family. He used all sorts of people to say a kind word, give us a few dollars, or invite us to dinner. Once a lady came by the apartment and told me that the Lord sent her over. She gave us $800.00 cash to pay our rent and a back car note. The day before the sheriff came by to inform us that our furniture would be put out on the street because we had not paid our rent. We had one day to get the money. Michael, Andrea, and I prayed together with tears in our eyes. We believed God could send a raven through the window with the money if He so willed. He sent that woman as our raven! Praise God for His goodness! There are no words to describe how we suffered, but through it all the Lord was faithful and our great provider: "Many are the afflictions of the righteous, but the Lord delivers him out of them all" (Psalm 34:19). After suffering for fourteen months, the Lord began to open the doors again. In October 1988 Michael got his job back as a math specialist with Detroit Public Schools. I was able to get a job as a part-time teller at NBD bank. Things started to look better financially.

During our severe trials, the Lord sent us to a large Baptist church in Livonia, Michigan to serve. In December 1989, my father died. Two months later on February 19, 1990, my infant son Andre D'Juan died. He was born prematurely and lived only a few hours. Grief overtook me. I felt as if I couldn't go on. I wanted to die. But, deep in my heart I knew God was with me and that He would see me through this difficult time: "God is our refuge and strength, a very present help in trouble" (Psalm 46:1). At first I was in shock. I did not believe God would let my child die. Not me, for I felt that my faithfulness to God should count for something. After all, didn't I trust Him for my every need? Didn't I praise Him for all the good things He had done for me? Out of all the people in the world, why my child? My only son? Hadn't I suffered enough in this life? It was during this time that I learned to praise the Lord in the good times and in the bad times. "I will bless the Lord at all times. His praise shall continually be in my mouth" (Psalm 43:1). Just because I was dedicated to the Lord would not exempt me from suffering. Some of God's greatest leaders had to suffer greatly.

In 1990, things were going pretty good financially and spiritually. Michael was now a deacon, missions committee leader, and Sunday school teacher. I was a leader in the Awana Program and a Sunday school teacher. Our jobs were secure. Michael felt it was time to save for a home. I went along with the plan, even though in my heart I felt it was foolish to think we would secure a loan for a home. After all, I was now an assistant manager at NBD bank, and I was familiar with the type of financial portfolio a client had to have to get a house. Our credit rating was very bad. During our trial in 1987, our payments to all our creditors were late. In God's wisdom we realized that the Bible said, "Owing nothing to anyone except to love one another" (Romans 13:8). We went back to all we owed and paid our debts, even when the creditors had already written us off.

In September of 1990, Michael took me to this beautiful new subdivision. The houses were very expensive. They were the kind people dreamed about. He told me he felt the Lord would allow him to have one of those houses built for our family. I laughed at him. I told him there was no way we could ever afford to purchase a home such as the models we saw. Deep in my heart, I wanted one of those houses in that beautiful subdivision. I was angry with Michael for even taking me to see those houses when he knew we wouldn't afford them. I prayed for a full week to the Lord that He would either give me the means to get this dream home or take the desire of the house from me. The desire never left me. Was I becoming too materialistic? Why would God allow such a wonderful blessing to happen to me anyway? I didn't deserve it. I felt guilty for wanting something so nice. The house had three bedrooms, 2-1/2 bathrooms, a kitchen with a kitchen nook, formal dining room, living room, laundry room, and, to top all that, a loft area that overlooked the family room with a fireplace. How could this all come true?

In May 1991, the time had come to build the new home. Michael took a step of faith and put a small amount down for the down payment. We didn't even have all the down payment money. The Lord blessed miraculously with all the down payment money. There were many more trials we experienced while the house was being built, but the Lord saw us through them all. In January 1992, we finally moved into our new home. My dream home! Who would have thought that this minister's wife, the little confused girl from Roseville, Michigan would grow up to have a home such as this. After all the suffering and pain the Lord had a plan for me, Jeremiah 29:11: "For I know the plans that I have for you, declares the Lord, plans for welfare and not for calamity to give you a future and a hope." Jesus wants us to surrender our lives to Him, and in due time He will exalt us. "If anyone wishes to come after me, let him deny himself, and take up his cross and follow me. For whoever wishes to save his life shall lose it, but whoever loses his life for My sake shall find it. For what will it profit a man it he gains the whole world and forfeits his soul" (Matt 16:24-26).

With all the good things that had come his way, it's no wonder you could hear Job saying, "the Lord giveth and He taketh away, but I'll still give Him thanks." For when the tables were all turned around and Job's world came crashing down, his faith in God told Job to say, "I'll still give Him thanks."

When troubles come and there's no one around, Satan tries to tell you, "God's let you down," but, in every dark hour, the best thing I've found is to give God the thanks. For he has never, never, failed me yet, so why should I start now to worry or fret, in everything don't ever forget to give God the thanks. In the good times, praise His name. In the bad times, do the same. In every thing, give the King of Kings all the thanks.

"In Everything Give Thanks," by the Brooklyn Tabernacle Choir, was the song Dave and sang at the funeral of the Thomases' son, André. They requested the same song to be song at the dedication of their new home. We live in a world where many feel they have a right to name and claim anything they desire. God is not Santa Claus. Put the "S" at the end and spelled backwards, Santa becomes Satan. Millions sell themselves short by seeking merely the gifts and forget seeking the best--the Giver.

The Thomases' greatest desire was seeking God's kingdom, "Seek ye first the kingdom of God and His righteousness, all these things shall be added unto you" (Matthew 6:33). As for the things, far too often people get things, and it's these very things that keep them from the things of God. It would damage their new car to make small trips for the needs of the elderly. Their house, opening it for the ministry of hospitality, would be unheard of. "Beloved, I wish above all things that thou mayest prosper and be in health, even as thy soul prosper" (III John 2).

The Thomases' 1987 trial was at its peak in 1988 when Dave and I left on our first faith's journey into South Africa. They knelt with us in prayer. They also wanted to share in a tangible way. How could they when they had so little? The week before we left, they prayed and gave us their last $10. There was no money in their savings account. They had no checking account. How foolish a gesture the natural man would say. What would the natural man say, seeing them today? Their seeking the kingdom didn't stop there. Today as we are preparing for work in South Africa, they were two of the first to be a part of our support team with a monthly financial commitment. The natural man would reply, "why you have a new mortgage to pay and furnishings to get for the house." The response is different when you know the truth of God's word which says, "Give, and it shall be given unto you: good measure, press down, shaken together, and running over, shall men give into your bosom. For with the same measure, that ye measure withall, it shall be measured unto you" (Luke 6:38). "But my God shall supply all your need according to His riches in glory by Christ Jesus" (Philippians 4:19).

The Thomases shared a testimony that dreams do come true and prayers are answered by an almighty, all loving, sovereign God, who alone is worthy to receive all the glory. No one can beat God giving! But you say, what about all of their dreams? Yes, two years later, almost to the date, a beautiful baby boy was born. His mother had a history of drug abuse. She was also

Arlene's sister. The baby was to be placed in temporary foster care. "Why certainly Arlene would take the baby," the family members cried. The Lord worked in the Thomas family's heart. There were many fears to overcome: perhaps the child would have cocaine addition symptoms; what if the biological mother desired to have her child back after the Thomases endeavored to put so much of themselves into his life and he into theirs? It would be like losing another son? **What if....** became replaced with a very great truth recorded over and over again in the Bible. **But God...**

Two years later, the Thomases are thoroughly enjoying the reality of their dreams. Unfortunately, the biological mother, when discovered missing for some period, was found dead. "Be not deceived; God is not mocked; for whatsoever a man soweth, that shall he also reap. For he that soweth to the flesh shall of the flesh reap corruption; but he that soweth to the Spirit shall of the Spirit reap life everlasting" (Gal. 6:7-8).

At the funeral service, Michael had an opportunity to include in the eulogy I Cor. 15:55-57: "O death, where is thy sting? O grave, where is thy victory? The sting of death is sin; and the strength of sin is the law. But thanks be to God, which giveth us the victory through our Lord Jesus Christ." Perhaps unknowingly, the sister had chosen a very appropriate name for her son—Emmanuel, which is interpreted, God with us. Romans 8:28 became a reality to the Thomases again, "And we know that all things work together for good to them that love God, to them who are the called according to His purpose."

FOR DISCUSSION:

#1   In an age of "name it and claim it" and chasing the god of prosperity, how can one truly differentiate between seeking the Giver and not the gift?

#2   Are you aware Satan knows how to give good gifts as well (Matt. 4: 8-9)?

#3   List some of the dreams and desires you wish to come true.

#4 "No good thing will He withhold from them that walk uprightly" (Psalm 84:11). Do you believe this? Perhaps why haven't some of your dreams come true?

#5 What should happen if we prosper and our hearts are turned from God? How can we avoid receiving abundantly and forgetting things which are really important?

Chapter Twelve

Chapter Twelve
HE LOOKED BEYOND MY FAULTS

by Terylle Lavender

My name is Terylle. I am a 30 year-old wife and mother. With my four sisters and one brother, I was born and raised in Kalamazoo, Michigan by my mom and step-father. As I remember my childhood years, I recall always having the things we needed. My mom had experienced severe poverty in her childhood. She and my step-father worked very hard to make sure we had adequate food, clothing, and housing. I learned later of the severe poverty she experienced in her childhood. It was also a tough job being a step-father.

Two of my sisters and I loved to dance and sing, and we would practice while my mom was at work. When she and my dad got home, we would perform for them. I also remember giving them private gymnastic shows because Mom had provided lessons for me. I recall trips to the beach and visits to friends (who were like family); Christmas caroling around the tree; and working summers; camping trips, and days sitting around playing "Concentration - concentration ready begin... thinking of (clap, clap) names of...," and, then, it seems as though overnight things changed.

Life was not fun and carefree anymore. I had to make decisions, and I didn't know how. My feelings were changing; my thoughts were changing; my needs were changing. It seemed my whole world was different, and I couldn't figure it out. Good communication between me and my parents about these changes did not exist; they did not understand me, and I did not understand them. I really felt the need to be understood. I needed someone to explain to me what was going on inside of me and help me adjust and deal with these changes. I realize now that my parents did the best they could with what they knew. They had both come from dysfunctional homes, and they did not know the Lord at this time.

I didn't have a relationship with my biological father. I really don't remember missing this when I was young, but over the past few years I've realized just how much I was affected by not being able to process the absence of my biological father. As a result of the breakdown in relationships at home, my mom gave me the choice of leaving. I was seventeen years-old when I left on August 17, 1979. Finally, I thought I would be free to be me and I could do all the things I wanted to do, answering to no one. This turned out to be one of the worst times in my life because I lost everything. To my surprise, I soon learned that my boyfriend didn't love me. I felt as though I had lost my home, and I had lost myself. At first I had lots of "friends" around, and we (at least I) drank and "got high" to escape reality. I quit going to school, although I tried to continue, but failed with every attempt. It was as though I had no drive. In shame and disbelief at not earning my high school diploma, on graduation night I determined to go to adult education and get my GED. I completed that program in August of 1980, just three months after graduation.

I was so very lonely, bitter, and angry that often times I cried myself to sleep, and wanted to commit suicide. I think what I really wanted was to do something with myself so that someone would know I was alive, and be truly interested in me. The boys just wanted me for one thing--sex. I wanted so badly to be special to someone. I still get tears in my eyes just to think of those desperate, lonely days and nights.

As kids, my parents sent us to different churches, but I don't ever remember really hearing the Gospel. I can't imagine the wrath God has for ministers who Sunday after Sunday never present the Good News; hundreds walk out of their congregations unsaved. I do remember after going to a Catholic church and catechism classes I began to have a hunger for God. I had heard that Jesus died for the sins of the world, but I never heard that He died for mine personally, or that I needed to believe and confess Him as Lord and Savior in order to be saved.

In 1980, my parents became Christians through the ministry of Bible Baptist Church, and they began inviting me to attend. I did. After hearing the Gospel message, I accepted Christ as my Savior in the Fall of 1981, and followed Him in believers' baptism on November 9, 1981. I attended Sunday school, worship services and a Bible class at the church, but soon left my first Love. "As a dog returns to its vomit, so a fool repeats his folly" (Proverbs 26:11). Back out into the world I went, only to regress worse than before. This time, however, I didn't fit in, and there was something within that never let me forget that I didn't belong.

My sister and I lived together at this time, and we had been through a lot together. She was very encouraging of me when I first got saved and seemed to be proud of the changes she saw in me. She was sad to see me give up on living like a Christian, even though she was not a believer. In late Summer of 1982, I went to Chicago to visit my cousins. I was really taken in by the bright lights and fast-moving cars and trains. There were so many people around. I didn't care that they weren't close to me. It was enough just to have so many people everywhere. I decided to secure a job in the city. I came back to Kalamazoo, gave two week's notice, and in October, 1982 I moved to Chicago.

I was a little afraid at first, but I thank God for some of those fears. I had drunk alcoholic beverages and used marijuana, but, when I got to the City, I was so afraid that there might be something lethal in the drugs, so I stopped. My life had been touched by relatives and friends who had fallen prey to the devil's lie about drugs. Drugs are a horrible web, sapping the very life of individuals so caught. I know that "but for the Grace of God, there go I."

After being in Chicago for almost three years, I met a guy. I had lived a promiscuous life since I was sixteen years-old, and it didn't take long before I was buying the devil's lie that premarital sex can provide a happy, fulfilling lifestyle, filling emptiness. What a lie!!! I was doing my own thing, and, at first, the guy seemed to be nice. As I got to know him a little better, I realized we did not have the same interests. But it was too late. I was pregnant. I did things a bit backwards; we do that when we go our own way. "There is a way that seems right to a (woman) but the end thereof is destruction." I don't remember the date, but I do remember the moment. I sat on my couch by the window and cried out, "Lord, I know you didn't cause this to happen. I did. I don't know what You are saying to me, but I know that whatever Your will is for my life, I want it . Please forgive me. I'm afraid. Please show me the way to go."

Soon after, my mom called. The Lord had already burdened her heart with my need for her. When I accepted the fact that I was going to be on my own with a baby, I called my parents and asked them to help me move home. They came, picked me up, and brought me back--no questions asked.

My mom and I began to talk about my relationship with the Lord, and I began to go to church. The Lord was really doing a work in my heart. I lay in bed one night at my sister's house, and my heart was really aching. I was missing the father of my child and was really hurt because he was denying me and the baby. How I hated rejection. I wrote him letters which he never answered. I couldn't understand why I had let this happen. That night, again I cried out to the Lord and I said, "I've said the right things, and I've believed that I meant them, but something is wrong. I've tried to live the Christian life, and I just don't know what else to do. You will just have to do it for me. I just don't know what else to do. You know my heart better than I do. You know if I have truly believed. Please help me." '"Faithful is He who calls you, and He also will bring it to pass" (I Thessalonians 5:24).

I had been attending Sunday school and church, and the Lord was specifically speaking to me. The Sunday school lessons were about carnality, and it seemed the Lord was saying, "I should be able to feed you meat, but you're still a babe. Therefore, I must give you milk." The carnal mind cannot be right with God, but something kept holding me back. Sunday after Sunday, I would say, "Lord, I can't go; I'm ashamed; I'm fat. People will think I'm just doing this because of my pregnancy. Lord, You will have to move me, and tell me what to say." Because of the things that happened to me in my past I didn't believe God loved me or anybody loved me. I wanted God to prove it to me before I believed Him. I was saved, and I had asked Him to take the hate and anger that was in my heart and replace it with love. Since I still had so much hate and anger, I didn't believe I really could be His child. God had already proved it at Calvary, but He was willing to show me even more if I could only believe and trust Him, not just as

Saviour, but also as Lord of my life. I confessed my sin, cried out to the Lord, and said that I didn't want to live the way I was living any more. This was the first time I remember publicly yielding my will to the Lord and giving Him Lordship of my life. At that very moment, it felt as though a weight had been lifted off me; I felt renewed. God's people put their arms around me. One sister was on her way down the isle before I had even finished talking. It was a day I will never forget because God's love was evidenced to me. He looked beyond my faults, saw my need, and forgave me. I knew He would never leave me, nor forsake me.

On February 14, 1985, at 2:00 a.m., I went into labor. I waited until daylight, and then my mom took me to the hospital. I remember Marjory Patrick calling me at the hospital to give me a verse to memorize. "Come unto me all you who labor and are heaven laden I will give you rest" (Matthew 11:28). I kept repeating this verse, but I also remember saying "soon give you rest." Her concern was encouraging. At 3:05 p.m., I was delivered of a baby girl, by cesarean section. My mom and younger sister named her "Yolanda" and I chose "Darlene" for the middle name, after my oldest sister.

The days ahead as a single mother would be hard, filled with many tears and heartaches, but also lots of joy and victory. We would pray about sleeping through the night, and other concerns which seemed bigger than life. I returned to school and trusted the Lord to provide and see me through. I had to learn to let go of the dream to be a complete family with my daughter's father. I thank God for the fellowship of the single adults at my church. They were very much family to "Yogi" and me. I also began to treasure and thank the Lord for my family who were very supportive from the beginning.

On May 22, 1985, Marjory and some of the women at the church started a group called "the victory club", as a time of fellowship and Bible study specifically for unwed mothers. Our theme verse was "we are more than conquerors through Him that loved us" (Romans 8:37).

Several of us unwed mothers came together. We were encouraged to keep a journal of our feelings and things that were happening in our lives. Literature relative to the needs, trials, and successes of the unwed mother was limited. Although several of us unwed mothers came together, it was difficult to find other Christian unwed mothers who were truly fighting this battle in the strength of the Lord. Marjory told us we would have to write the story. Writing in my journal really helped me deal with my feelings and to be honest with the Lord. We also had leadership responsibilities in the group which I think really helped because it made me feel useful and like one who could contribute in the Lord's work. The duties were also good for my low self-esteem.

The Lord used different people to help me deal with the anger and resentment I had toward the baby's father. He helped me to forgive him and to ask for His forgiveness for the willful sin which I had committed as a believer. Over a period of time, the Lord also helped me accept the fact of not having him in Yolanda's life and to trust HIM to be the Father of the Fatherless, which He promised to do. He gave me such a hunger for His Word and for fellowship with Him. He led me each day to read to "Yogi" and to pray through everyday situations. He provided everything we ever needed. I thank God for the people, His people, who were faithful and loved Him enough to help us as He led.

I thought I was doing okay in my walk with the Lord. I had spent a lot of time studying the Word, but I was very anxious for a husband. I wanted so badly to be married, and everyday I prayed, asking the Lord if this would be the day I would meet my husband. One day I met Lorenzo, who would eventually become my husband. I was so excited, and, before I knew it, I had taken things back into my own hands. I ran ahead of the Lord. I failed to trust Him once again.

Not long after we began dating, we got sexually involved. Once again, I was pregnant, and so afraid. I did not want to face my church congregation; they would think I really wasn't a Christian. I decided abortion was the only way out, so I could just pretend that it never happened. After the abortion, I continued in my immoral lifestyle. I wanted so badly to stop, but I felt as though I were powerless to do so. I tried breaking off the relationship, but I was "a silly woman, laden with sin, taken captive. Each is tempted when by (her) own evil desire, (she) is dragged away and enticed. Then, after desire has conceived, it gives birth to sin, and, sin, when it is full grown, gives birth to death" (separation, broken fellowship with God) (James 1:13-15).

In less than a year, I was pregnant again. Another abortion was my way out. I never dreamed I would make such decisions, nor did I realize the effect those decisions would have on my life for the next several years. Spiritually and emotionally distraught (a wreck), I was suicidal. I was certain I was going to lose my mind, but I didn't understand why. I didn't know that this dreadful sin in my life had to be dealt with because I was sure the Lord finally had thrown me away. He could never forgive me for such a thing as this. Or could He?

On June 17, 1989, I became Mrs. Lorenzo Lavender and the stepmother of his eleven year-old daughter, Aliah. When Lorenzo and I dated, Aliah and I had a great relationship, but, after we seriously contemplated marriage, our relationship began to fail. I failed to be the friend Aliah needed in me. I am now praying that all will be reconciled and the relationship will be restored.

The first month of marriage was wedded bliss, but the effects of sin began to take a toll. I hated Lorenzo, and I hated myself. I was angry about the abortions. How could I do such a thing? I tried not to let myself think about them so that the guilt would go away, but it didn't. I became pregnant again six months after the wedding, and I could not ignore my past any more. Constant reminders like pictures of aborted fetuses would remind me of what I had done.

On October 3, 1990, Lorenzo and I became the parents of a beautiful baby girl. We named her "Loren." During my "spare" time, I decided to go to the Crisis Pregnancy Center (CPC) and volunteer as an advisor to help someone else, and in that way I could make up for what I had done. Before this volunteer work, the Lord had been telling me to deal with the sin in my own life. I felt convicted by the Word, Bible reading, and sermons. I wanted to go to the leadership of my church and share what I had done, and I felt Lorenzo and I should go forward publicly and confess that we were sorry for this sin. Would the leadership respond in compassion? How would other believers respond? We never did make our sin public, but in our hearts we confessed to God.

I went to a training session at CPC, and we all had to introduce ourselves giving a reason why we were there. Before it was my turn to share, I kept going over in my head what I would say. I kept changing my thoughts, saying "no, I won't tell them"; I'll just say, "I want to help other girls because I was once a single parent." But the Lord had other things in mind. I believe now with all my heart that the Lord is HOLY! HOLY! HOLY! and requires that we deal with known sin in our lives, if we belong to Him. If we don't, He will. He gives us the opportunity to judge ourselves and come clean before Him, but if we don't, because He loves us, He must step in and chasten us. If we are not chasten, we are probably not one of His children. "For whom the Lord loveth He chasteneth, and scourgeth every son whom He receiveth" (Hebrews 12:6).

When I opened my mouth, the whole story came out. For the first time since the abortions, I was sharing with a room full of women the dreadful sin in my life. I could hardly talk, for sobbing. I truly was sorry not because I had gotten caught, but because I knew what I had done was sin against God. I had killed two of His children. I was a murderer. I was so afraid I would be judged by those women and rightly so. That night, a dear lady took me in her arms and just held me and let me cry. God used her arms to comfort me. I felt His love that night just as I did the Sunday I came forward and yielded my will to Him. I felt at peace with God. Then I went to a deaconess in my church, and she cried and held me and said she would pray for me.

About a year after the CPC counseling experience, I went to a post-abortion group counseling session. The Word of God says that when God forgives our sin, He throws it into the sea of forgetfulness and remembers it no more. He separates it from us as far as the East is from the West. "If we confess our sins, He is faithful and just to forgive us our sin, and cleanse us from all unrighteousness" (I John 1:9). It's true. God has not dealt with me according to my sin, but instead He has given me His grace and His mercy which endure forever and His peace which passes all understanding. He loved me while I was yet a sinner and knew the things I would do against Him; yet, He still died for me and saved me.

Today, I am still being conformed to the image of His precious Son. "I know in whom I have believed, and am persuaded that He is able to keep that which I have committed unto Him" (II Timothy 1:12). "I am confident of this very thing, that He who began a good work in me will perfect it until the day of Jesus Christ" (Phillipians 1:6).

Only by the grace of God, I am not living in willful sin. I have asked God to help me see myself as He sees me, "to search me and know my heart, try me and know my anxious thoughts, and see if there be any hurtful way in me and lead me in the everlasting way" (Psalm 139:23-24). He looks beyond my faults and sees my needs. My need, as I knew it, was to be special to someone and to be loved unconditionally. I've learned, and believed, through study of God's Word, through prayers and through trials that I am special to God. He alone can love me with an everlasting love. "Who shall separate me from the love of Christ? Shall trouble or hardship or persecution, or famine or nakedness or danger or sword? As it is written "For your sakes I face death all day long; I am considered as a sheep to be slaughtered. No, in all these things I am more than a conqueror through Him that loved me. For I am convinced that neither death nor life, neither angels nor demons, neither the present nor the future, nor any powers, neither height nor depth, nor anything else in all creation, shall be able to separate me from the love of God that is in Christ Jesus my Lord" (Romans 8:35-39).

"Be ye holy, for I am holy." Leviticus 11:45, Ephesians 1:4

Oh God, we are saddened by the number of young African-American women who become pregnant out of wedlock. A pregnancy wrought from the web of premarital sex occurs every thirty seconds, in the U.S. Four thousand infants are killed daily by means of abortion in the United States. God will not allow these acts to continue without judgment. He continues to call for genuine repentance and a turning away from such acts.

This section is written for girls and women everywhere as exhortation to flee youthful lust. If this chapter can prevent one more act of premarital and/or one less act of murder, then God will be glorified.

As Christian women, we have a responsibility to vote for people in Congress who can overthrow decisions treating life as mundane. We have to encourage our sons and daughters to see our sexuality as God designed it to be. We have to foster the priority of life which God has always placed on it. "The fruit of the womb is His reward" (Psalm 127:3). This is not to voice against family planning, unless abortion is considered a method for birth control. That is morally wrong!

Somehow, we have lost sight of the awesome privilege of child bearing. Many enjoy putting down women who are "just" housewives. Rearing children is a lost art, and a mother's care-giving of her own children is thought to be second class. Only as we begin valuing our own children, will we begin valuing ourselves and stop yielding ourselves to Satan's deceptions!

"What, know ye not that your body is the temple of the Holy Ghost. Ye are not your own. For ye are bought with a price: therefore, glorify God in your body, your spirit, which are God's" (I Corinthians 6:19-20).

"Let not therefore sin reign in your mortal body" (Romans 6:12). The finished work Christ wrought at Calvary paid the penalty for all of our past sins. It has power to save us from the practice of sin, and will one day soon save us from the very presence of sin. Keeping our hearts focused on the fact of Christ's return keeps us pure (I John 3:3).

The next time you are tempted to sin, think of Christ's second return. Take time to encourage another sister in Christ, "exhort (mentor, disciple) her to good works, and so much the more as you see the day approaching" (Hebrews 10:25).

He who is faithful and true said, "Behold I come quickly." He wishes to return for His bride without spot or wrinkle. "Even so, come Lord Jesus" (Revelation 22:20).

FOR DISCUSSION:

#1 Are you appalled by the anti-abortion leaflets showing the realities of abortion? Do you tune these out of your mind like changing the channels of a television horror movie?

#2 What concrete things can we as Christian women do in the fight against abortion? Remember, God will judge us not only for what we do, but also for what we fail to do!

#3 Far too many Christian women find themselves trapped in cycles of sexual sins. Spiritual strongholds occur from opportunities where Satan yet has a foothold in their lives. Deliverance is possible. Are you aware of individuals or pastors in your area who are equipped to help in a ministry such as this?

#4 How can we as Christians have a more reverential awe and fear of God in the area of our sexuality?

#5 How great is the impact of sexual sins in your community, in your local church? How great is move of believers in your area prepared to aggressively fight against this demonic spirit? Or whose son or daughter will be the next victim?

Chapter Thirteen

Chapter Thirteen
OH HOW I LOVE HIM SO

by Marjory Washington Patrick

While sitting by the bank of the Huron River one day, I was amazed at the creation of God and all His wonders. Funny, how sitting by a river, looking upwards towards the hills, gazing into a starry night, or into an infant's smile causes one to stop and be amazed at the awesomeness of God Almighty.

The sun light hit the waters just right. The wind caused the waters to ripple. I hummed, "Oh How I Love Him So...for taking my place at Calvary...", "If There Were No One Else He still would have died for me...", "Somebody Bigger Than You And I...", "Surely Goodness and Mercy...shall follow me all the days of my life...", "God Gave Me a Song that the angels can not sing..." -- all of these song titles and tunes from my past rang through my head, my heart, my soul.

As a child, our house was filled with music. There were very few days - no hours, that gospels, hymns, or spiritual songs did not ring in our home. From Mahaliah Jackson, Edwin Hawkins, George Beverly Shea, and the Jones Sisters, and other artist, to the sounds of our family - Daddy sang bass; Momma sang alto; brother sang tenor, and I sang soprano; baby sister sat pretty and smiled. We had a song for every occasion. We'd sing traveling in the car and we'd take deep breaths to see who could hold their notes the longest, go the highest, or roar the lowest. Those were fun times! Mother would also remind us of the importance of living the life we sang about.

I was loved a lot, and I knew it. So many failures of children apparently are a direct result of parents, and other significant others, not accepting children for who they are. I wasn't accepted for playing the piano, singing in church, winning national debate and forensic titles, and more. I was accepted for who I was--a creation of God sent by Him, entrusted to be a part of this particular family.

Inclusive in my parent's love and pride was an acceptance of my failures--the bed wetting, the bad eating habits, my meanness, and more. I wasn't left alone to decide "who I was." So many children aimlessly wander about wondering who they are, what is their purpose, and where are they going? Many parents think the child will just stumble upon his/her quest without being guided. Proverbs 6:22 gives a definite active command, "train up a child in the way he should go...." This includes training them in the course they are 'bent"--predispositioned to go. This means parents will have to take the time to really know the child, their temperament, their strengths and weaknesses. Bombarded in their desire to accumulate money and acquire things, many parents lose sight of really knowing and loving their children.

I loved my childhood. I loved the comfort of a solid family. It was a wondrous sight to walk through the quietness of a room and see my mother sitting communing with God, in the Word, and/or prayer. My father openly praised my mother. He never spoke harshly or cursed in our home. The day I drove a car into my father's car, right in our own driveway, I thought he would surely explode. No, he maintained control even then. I was disciplined later.

My mother instilled the pride we felt for our father. She was proud of him and it was obvious. He was Kalamazoo's first Black elected official. He also formed and directed a drum and bugle corps and sport leagues for the Black community. I recall many a time when he would bring in large bundles from the shoe store. "Boy dad, these are a lot of shoes for us!" But no, they were shoes he bought for those in the community who had none, so that they could participate in the programs he offered.

It was of great significance to me that my mother spoke praise and encouragement to our father. Even though she was quite busy in the music ministry of the church and the community and she worked and ministered at the Plainwell Mental Health Institution, she had time to participate in my father's endeavors. It seems that too many parents today think nothing of belittling one parent right in front of the children. So many children, so many spouses, live with constant criticism. Criticism kills.

Criticism kills the spirit, and thwarts the desire to achieve.

Criticism makes one defensive, and breeds a lack of self-worth.

Criticism makes one want to avoid the one who is criticizing.

Criticism makes one feel unloved, and rejected.

Criticism makes one feel insecure.

Criticism of one's talents stifles one's creative expression.

Criticism makes it difficult to receive compliments, and to accept love.

With our words, we either build or tear down. There is a difference between constructive criticism and criticism. Constructive criticism rebuilds the individual. As we "talk at," shout, nag, etc., we chip away at the very life threads of the individual. As we compliment, as we encourage, as we talk with individuals, we speak "life" into them.

In many households, there are too many instances of attacking, self-boasting, and very little building. Many don't know what it is like to speak words of encouragement into one another. Too often parents are building houses instead of building homes. I'm certain God longs on family altars to elicit praise in a world that is intent on tearing families apart. In fact, I'm sure God is looking for homes that still have a family altar.

My father also taught me the true meaning of a man's love. He would stand hours in the hot sun at one of my sister's ball games. He'd welcome into our home for weekends or holidays children from the social service group homes. Even in all this activity, I had a father who was there for ME. He occasionally would surprise me with small tokens. We went on dates to the mall or the park, and he would sit with me, putting together picture puzzles; we'd color in coloring books, or read news articles together. He never doubted that I would come home with the winning speech trophy, and, just in case I didn't (which was rare), it was okay because he made me feel I was acceptable as I was, and so I was always a winner!

I never wanted for the superficial love of men. How important it is for fathers to take time with their children. A daughter who is running from relationship to relationship is usually a daughter who is really longing for the lack of a relationship with her own father. A loving father/daughter relationship allows a woman to wait for just the right man/woman relationship, if that is God's ultimate plan for her life. Appropriate God-fearing father/daughter relationships can significantly reduce rampant teen/young adult sexual abuse. The right father/daughter relationship allows single women to live at levels of fulfillment which are rich. Not having husbands, they do not have to live feeling as though they are less than fulfilled women. Even though many fathers are not modeling the role as God intends, Christ is our ultimate Example. One must look to Him to fulfill all one's needs. We must pray earnestly for our men. When was the last time you spent a "sweet hour of prayer" for some special men in your life? Women often are the ones leading family devotions and encouraging the family to attend church. Many a child has been won to the Lord by a mother on her knees.

My mother and I had many good talks and times of interaction before her death. This really impressed upon my mind the need to redeem the time because one never knows what tomorrow will bring. After a long battle with cancer, the Lord called His servant, home to take her rest: "Blessed are the dead which die in the Lord from henceforth: yea, saith the Spirit, that they may rest from their labors: and their works do follow them" (Revelation 14:13).

Most vividly, I remember my mother spending TIME with individuals. I'd often go along to keep her company. Perhaps

I'd get to baby-sit, which I so enjoyed. I'd keep an infant or toddler occupied in order for my mother to freely minister. When I was fourteen, I sat building blocks with little Kenny. In the background, I could hear his mother say, "if only I had given my life to the Lord at Marjie's age, I'd have more of my life to live for Him." She cried, "too many wasted years, too many wasted years." These words echoed in my heart and were impressed upon my soul – today while you are young, give your life to the Lord. Witness now. Read the Bible. Don't be like so many adults who regret that they have yet to read God's Word all the way through; they have yet to lead someone else to the Lord. That evening, I went home and in my bedroom committed my whole life to the Lord. I was determined to read God's Love Letter to me from cover to cover. I began witnessing at school. I had pen pals all over the U.S. whom I would write to tell about God's love. I left Gospel leaflets whenever I had opportunity. I attended all the services at church, not because my parents insisted, but because I wanted to be there. I helped at Vacation Bible School and the Circle Y Ranch, a Christian camp. There was JOY in serving Jesus.

I have always loved church. Our family grew up in a traditional Black Baptist church. Once, some friends and I were playing church in our house. One of the boys could copy the tone, roaring, and rocking exactly like the sermon heard on Sunday; he played the part of the preacher. One of the girls played the part of the sister who could shout the loudest, and then be carried out by the ushers. I got to sing the Sunday morning solo. I wanted to sing just like Jean Morris because of her gift of music. Somewhere within some of our people, I'm certain there was pure sincerity, and not all show, but sometimes I felt it was show because I didn't see lifestyles Monday through Saturday that matched what I heard on Sundays.

Controversies of styles of worship do exist. Some people are uncomfortable with charismatic emotionalism. Some of these same people don't consider themselves too charismatic at ball games, or other sporting events shouting at the top of their voices, jumping, and waving for their sport heroes. Certainly the Lord of Lords and Captain of our Salvation is worthy to be praised! Amen and Hallelujah!!! I am saddened by the fact that this phenomenon--charismatic confusion-versus cold, dead fundamentalism--divides genuine believers. I am saddened that our expressions of worship can be masked as mere emotional releases. God desires that our praise be in Spirit and in Truth. I long for the time when all the saints will gather and have shouts of praise to the Lamb that was slain; we won't have to worry who might object to our falling at His feet! Needless to say, I don't mind enjoying some of that kind of worship here and now.

My parents joined with a group of believers who hungered for more than mere emotional expressions, and a fundamental Black Bible church was formed. I could see a difference in the formative years of this Bible church, and we kids no longer wanted to play church based on what we experienced. The new Black fundamental church went through persecution. I saw others, including my mother, spat upon and tongue lashed for the sake of the Gospel. There were lashings from other Black people accusing us of being "Uncle Toms," promoting a white man's religion.

I remember walking in on adult conversations and hearing talk of the mass of white fundamental churches across the United States where Truth was taught, supposedly unadulterated, but Blacks preparing for the ministry were not admitted. Later, as discrimination dwindled racism continued and the white fundamental churches and their Sunday bus programs could accomplish little. This harvest was, indeed, plentiful, but most of the crop became rotten crop, unable to be harvested and now manifest itself in hideous inner city crime and ghetto gang wars.

We, as fundamentalists, were becoming full of the Word, but many of us got lost in Bible toting/quoting, forgetting to exhibit the fruits of the Spirit, even with one another. Somewhere forgotten was the mandate of God, "to whom much is given much is required" (Luke 12:48). Fundamental Christianity was not designed to be a platform from which white supremacy could flow; neither was it designed to be a platform from which spiritual superiority could initiate. If the Enemy can be allowed entrance into our churches to accomplish one of the things he does best--divide, white against white, white against Black, Black against Black, he is running his program well. When Satan and his host did enough damage here, and/or some of us woke up to this scheme and began integrating our churches and ourselves and goals, we conquered back some of the territory we lost.

So then Satan said to his host, let's increase or efforts to divide believers denominationally, especially between those who are "Evangelical" and "Charismatic." Satan knew mere knowledge of the Word for the sake of knowledge would puff up (I Cor. 1:8). He also knew that an imbalance spiritual experience would have believers so worn out that there would be little power for living victoriously daily. We can't afford to lose sight of our high calling to preach Christ and Him crucified. As He is lifted up He can draw all men to Himself. When we lift up ourselves, the world stands back mocking at the mess we've made. All our focus should be on Him, the study of His Word, obedience, and living out His Word, in love.

A traditional minister told me if I just got baptized, I could sing in the junior choir. What a tragedy! It was during these turbulent transitional times, that I came to know the Lord. Through Bible study and the ministry of a missionary to the Philippines, I came to know for myself that I was a sinner in God's sight, that Christ was my Substitute, and that He paid the penalty for my sins. By accepting His finished work, I had the right and joy of being God's child, "But as many received Him, to them gave He the power to become the sons of God, even to them that believe on His name" (John 1:12).

In November, 1965, I realized that I didn't have to guess or trust in my feelings or emotions. I knew I had eternal life: "There is only one life to live and it will soon pass; only what's done for Christ will last." The truth of that phrase sunk into my heart. It sunk in as a result of the life my mother lived because personal Bible study and fellowship with believers were a part of her everyday experience. Even today, I don't understand "Christians" who don't hunger for Bible study and Christian fellowship/worship. Some can barely make it to God's house on Sunday, and they completely forget Sunday night or mid-week Bible and prayer opportunities. Pastors and church leaders have to beg for participation in visitation programs.

I am grateful for the example I was shown by my mother and other Christian women. They showed me the awesome responsibility mothers have and the need for more Spirit-filled fathers to come to the rescue, not to lessen a mother's responsibility, but to equalize the influence. God has always called men to stand and take positions as prophets, priests, and kings in the home, in love and submission to an almighty Heavenly Father. Satan knows that a home under this kind of godly order is powerful! He has managed to dupe many women into believing they are the only ones able. This self-sufficiency, especially among African-American women, is destroying our relationships, and effectiveness as a people. Satan has duped our men into no longer believing God, who says we, as believers, are more than conquerors. African- American men need to "put on the whole armor of God in order to stand against the wiles of the devil" and rise to positions of spiritual leadership in the home and churches, as God intended. May we as women stand <u>beside our men</u>, not on, or under, or over, but <u>beside</u> them, realizing God is Able!!

After graduating from college, I married a wonderful Christian man, and we grew together spiritually in a white fundamental church. I praise the Lord for the growth and fellowship in Him, and I still hunger for the Black Christian fellowship I once knew because I do find joy in the fact that God first made me Black, with the cultural distinctives and soul derived with Blackness. Some believe there are no differences and that God doesn't see color. I do not think this is true. What is true, I believe, is that God is no respecter of persons, and we are one in Christ Jesus. "Man looks on the outward appearance, but God looks on the heart"(1 Samuel 16:7). God has a divine, magnificent purpose for creating each of us unique and as collective people groups. He has wonderfully orchestrated a symphony of people groups for His glory! In our own ways, we went astray.We became busy placing value upon our differences, instead of accepting and celebrating our differences.

The experiences of serving in a predominantly white church were many, but one of the things I remember most was the loneliness. Bonnie, a white sister, was used of the Lord to show me the difference He can make in relationships. Why couldn't

I be close to these Caucasian sisters? For one thing, I had sheltered myself. I would not open up or allow fellowship. I had been conditioned not to speak to white people first because they would only reject me. I never felt inferior but did feel that since whites didn't want me in their world, I wouldn't enter. hite fears of my Blackness somehow contaminating their white world sickened me and caused me to build even thicker walls.

Somehow, Bonnie and I reached to one another through those walls and we became friends. It was difficult to process and erase treatment of discrimination and prejudice of the past. Many whites feel, "why can't the past be forgiven and why can't Blacks stop blaming all whites for the root and problems of the past?" I tried forgetting scenes from secondary school where most of my interracial conflicts occurred. Even during college days in the 70's, I was placed in a dorm room with three white roommates; their parents feared for them having a Black roommate. This and numerous other experiences only added depth to the walls I was building around my heart.

I began to stop questioning God for His placement of us as an African-American couple in a white church. Just as I look in a mirror each morning and don't question why the nose on my face is a part of my body, I began to see God's placement of each individual believer into whatever local body of believers He so sovereignly desired.

My husband was a bus pastor of one of the largest Black routes. Many church members felt all Blacks were like the children on the routes-- wild, undisciplined, poverty-stricken, and in need of the transformation that only white people could give. Seven years after many walls of racism and fears were torn down, God gave us new directions, and a job transfer relocated us. The bus program was halted. I feel because it no longer fit the budget, or maybe it wasn't the "white" thing to do. How I was saddened years later, while working in one of Michigan's correction facilities, to see serving a life sentence, one of the young persons who was left without that bus ministry. If we could only get away from our staring and start sharing, we'd have churches not merely existing, but exhibiting the power of God in love, and about the business of building His Kingdom.

In 1988 when my husband, Dave, and I traveled to South Africa, many were understanding that apartheid is, fundamentally in its very nature, evil, immoral, and un-Christian. Our pastor, a white Messianic Jew, presented the gospel message in Bible conferences in all four of South Africa's major people groups, white, Black, colored, and Indian. Dave and I ministered in music alongside of him. A healing took place in the lives of many Christians to see us minister together. After being involved in several meetings in one day, it was wonderful to see at the close of an evening service all the races worshipping and fellowshipping together under the same roof. This scene helped me glimpse afresh a scene much like what John recorded in the Book of The Revelation. There was a population no man could number, from every tribe, every nation, every people group, gathered around the Throne. They weren't glorying in their whiteness, their blackness, their gold, or how much oil they possessed or their church affiliation; instead, they sang "Worthy is the Lamb!"

Now, in preparing for a missionary ministry in South Africa, we long to see white greed and superiority and Black oppression and aggression superseded by the love and unity of Christ. In writing this book, I have come to also want this for America. I am thrilled to have been a part of congregations who accept people groups as unique, special, and one in Christ. I also yearn to see spiritual healing among African-American women and healing between African-American men and women.

That day, I sat by the bank of the Huron River (in Ann Arbor, MI), was the day God impressed upon my heart, I wasn't loving Him the way I should. This was evident by the way I responded to my husband. God did a work in my heart that day, removing the selfish, stony heart I had, replacing it with a heart that could reflect the great love, God Himself, has for my husband. I found myself loving my husband to a degree I had never experienced. This love began to empower him to be all that God intends. I began to sense anew the hurt and pain of so many African-American men. The hurt and the pain stem from a root of rejection and torn self-actualization. I realized the potential, the power, the love of God which is truly transforming. The love of God, through us, can make a difference.

Years ago, Dr. Mary McLeod Bethune stated, "I would not exchange my color for all the wealth in the world. We have given something to the world as a race, and for this we are proud and fully conscious of our place in the total picture of mankind's development." We must learn to share, and mix with all mankind.

There continues to be a challenge to me, my daughters, and all Christian African-American women numbered among believers of all colors everywhere, to love the Lord with all our hearts, minds, and souls. In loving Him, we are able to love others who are different than ourselves. In loving Him, we are able, as African-American women, to love our African-American men so that they can be all that God intended. In loving Him, we can be the Christian African-American women Christ will be pleased to call to Himself upon His return. Oh, how I love Him so!

As my love for the Lord deepened, then the love for my husband also deepened. Love is not just a four letter word. Love expresses itself in how we live and respond to one another. This was one of the greatest lessons I had to learn before we embarked on a ministry together in South Africa. The other lessons we learned were just as great. These lessons I hope to share in Volume II, "Reflections of the South African Christian Woman of Color." Besides I want you to meet some of my newly found friends who also have a story to tell to the nations!

DISCUSSION QUESTIONS:

#1 In areas where we have been divided as Christians (race, gender, denominations/worship styles, etc. Do you see improvements?

#2 Much is spoken these days about traditional families and non-traditional families. (we use to call them broken families but not in an era of speaking politically correct) What do these families have in common?

#3   Much focus has been on the family. Have family values changed? What roles does each family member play in God's economy?

#4   If unity is important to God (John17:21) how do we practically strive for it in our homes, in our churches, internationally?

#5   This chapter title states, O how I love Him, John 14:15 tells us, "If ye love me, keep my commandments." Perhaps something you have read in one of these chapters will challenge you to have a greater love for the Lord increasing your obedience to Him. Take opportunity to share this challenge with someone you may be sharing this book with and together march on to victory!

Chapter Fourteen
YE ARE "A LIVING EPISTLE"

By You!

"Ye are our epistle written in our hearts, known and read of all men." (II Corinthians 3:2)

SAMPLE BIRTH CERTIFICATE

BIRTH CERTIFICATE

THIS IS TO CERTIFY

that
_____

was Born Again by receiving Jesus Christ as Personal Savior

on the _____ day of
_____ 19___
This acceptance of Christ was certified

by
_____

Take time to write and secure to your own heart the events and paths which lead to your becoming a Christian. Take time to write and leave for family and friends a legacy worth remembering...Your testimony!

Other Robbie Dean Press Publications having Christian Messages

One Split Second by Suzan Bryan Hoppe (a mother's poignant and, sometimes, humorous, yet always, spiritually uplifting story about her son's, her family's, and her own coping with traumatic brain injuries)

> This work is a remarkable statement of human struggle and faith. The book is honest, direct, and, therefore, powerful. —Robert Shaw, D.D., former Executive Minister, American Baptist Churches of Michigan

> Suzan Hoppe has recorded her journey through family catastrophe and tragedy with such honest and passion that the reader will share her growth from despair to hope and triumph. It...is a source of inspiration for all who struggle with the unfairness of life's circumstances. I recommend it highly.—Rev. Diana Goudie, Azalia & London United Methodist Churches

> Every person who has children should read this book. Every person who is facing or has overcome a major challenge can relate to this author's story.—Mrs. Willie Glaze, member of Second Baptist Church, Ann Arbor, MI

ISBN: 0-9630608-3-X: 15.00 (shipping and handling included)

Sermons By Sorors edited by Arlene H. Young (a collection of sermons by female ministers which touches upon the various challenges all people face)

> [Ms.] Young remained steadfast in her charge--being obedient to the Word--professional publication of a book.... The charge to make this publication a reality was out of her control; she knows that she was simply obedient; "...all that the Lord hath said will we do, and be obedient" (Exodus 24:6). —Bertha Maxwell Roddey, Ph.D., Immediate Past President of Delta Sigma Theta Sorority, Inc.

ISBN: 0-9630608-6-4; 12.50 (shipping and handling included)

Send check or money order to: *Robbie Dean Press*, 2910 E. Eisenhower Parkway, Ann Arbor, MI 48108

Celebrating 7 Years--Chronology of Publications

'91; '92; '94--**Essential Writing Skills for Deaf Students**, 2nd ed. by Fairy C. Hayes-Scott, Ph.D.--ISBN: 0-9630608-2-1--$25

'93; '94; '96--**Bare Essentials: An English Handbook for Beginner Writers**, 3rd ed. by Fairy C. Hayes-Scott--0-9630608-2-1--$25

'93--**Deaf/Blindness: Essential Information for Families, Professionals, & Students** by Isabell Florence--0-9630608-4-8--$12

'93--**One Split Second** (a mother's poignant and sometimes humorous story about her son's and her coping with traumatic brain injuries) by Suzan Bryan Hoppe--0-9630608-3-X--$15

'95--**Enter My World of Freighters...Photos on Display** by Vernon Sondak--0-9630608-5-6--$50

'95; '96; '97; '98--**International Journal for Teachers of English Writing Skills** (4 X a year with 3 newsletters)--ISSN: 1081-6364--$40 ind'ls; $50 indl's (abroad); $50 institutions; $60 inst. (abroad)

'96; '97-- **Narratives of ESL Students...The World Is Round**, 2nd ed. by Michael McColly--1-889743-00-3--$20

'96--**Sermons By Sorors** (an inspirational work; a collection of sermons by female ministers) ed. by Arlene H. Young--0-9630608-6-4--$12.50

'96--**The Teacher's Handbook of Multicultural Games Children Play** ed. by Shannon Murphy--0-9630608-9-9--$21

'97--**The African-American/Black Diaspora Word Search Puzzlebook** (more than a puzzlebook--a quick resource with an extensive biography providing information on more than 1500 individuals) by Benoit Tshiwala--1-889743-04-6--$25, add $4 (s&h)

'97--**Your Remarkable Anatomy** (this clearly illustrated book is for the layperson, ages 12+, and professional) by Dr. Don Lowell Fisher--1-889743-01-1--$25

'97; '98--**Parents Imparting Discipline & Heritage** ed. by Fairy C. Hayes-Scott with Nora Martin, Ph.D., consultant--1-889743-03-8--$25

'98--**Reflections of Christian Women** by Marjory Washington Patrick--1-889743-06-2--$12.50

Upcoming in March '99--**Facilitated Communication--Case Studies: Seeing Us Smart!** (a book detailing successsful methods for teaching autistic children) by Charlene Brandl

Upcoming in September '99--**The Values Computer Word Search Puzzlegame;** (this computer game is for children 4-8; **the 1st computer word search puzzlegame for children which teaches values!**) developed by Cheyne R. Scott--CD only--Mac or PC--$19.95

The above prices apply if the customer orders directly from the publisher.
Shipping & Handling included unless otherwise noted.
Profits from several of the above go to scholarships and other charitable donations.

Robbie Dean Press; 2910 E. Eisenhower Pkwy.; Ann Arbor, MI 48108
(734) 973-9511; fax--(734) 973-9475; FairyHa@aol.com
http://www.bookmasters.com/RobbieDeanPress